Budget Happy

Lisa Woodley is a married mother of three and grandmother of two who is passionate about educating people about money and breaking down taboos around budgeting. Lisa started posting her cash stuffing journey at the beginning of 2022 as a way to document her own budgeting and make herself accountable, but soon her profile blew up; it currently stands at over **166k followers** and is gaining hundreds more each day.

Budget Happy

THE WIN-WIN SECRET TO SAVING AND SPENDING MONEY

LISA WOODLEY

QUERCUS

First published in Great Britain in 2023 by

QUERCUS

Quercus Editions Ltd
Carmelite House
50 Victoria Embankment
London EC4Y 0DZ

An Hachette UK company

A CIP catalogue record for this book is available
from the British Library

HB ISBN 978 1 52943 046 2
Ebook ISBN 978 1 52943 048 6

Some names and identifying details have been changed to protect the privacy of individuals.

Every effort has been made to contact copyright holders.
However, the publishers will be glad to rectify in future
editions any inadvertent omissions brought to their attention.

Illustrations by Amber Anderson.

10 9 8 7 6 5 4 3 2 1

Typeset by CC Book Production
Printed and bound in Great Britain by Clays Ltd, Elcograf S.p.A.

Papers used by Quercus are from well-managed forests and other responsible sources.

This book is dedicated to my beautiful family:
Nick, Lacey, Ava and Poppy.

Contents

Introduction

'Budget' is not a dirty word. It isn't a party pooper, a school detention or a ball and chain around our ankles. So why is it that, when we think of budgeting, we immediately feel restricted and deprived, when in fact it is a positive, practical way to manage our finances? Everyone can benefit from embracing a budget, no matter how much money they may or may not have because, as we know, life has a habit of throwing scary curve balls, like a pandemic, cost-of-living crisis, threat of war, soaring interest rates and energy bills – and that doesn't include the difficult personal battles that may affect us too. Which is why being responsible for things within our power is a vital and – believe it or not – fun process. Yes, I did just say fun in relation to money management!

I want to banish the stigma surrounding budgeting and show you how to be in control of your money, rather than it being in control of you. Not only will it revolutionize your relationship with your bank account, but it will also be an enjoyable and rewarding experience. You won't be attempting complicated sums, updating spreadsheets or understanding the financial market; you just need a few envelopes and a plan of how to divide your money up to get started. It is a simple equation of saving to spend.

This is not a book that will tell you how to make more money. This is a straightforward strategy to help you make the most of what you already have, written by someone who has learned the hard way. I had a toxic money mindset for the first forty-ish years of my life until I discovered the practice of 'cash stuffing', a way of putting notes and coins aside for expenses, rather than relying on credit cards. I posted a video of my first cash stuffing exercise on TikTok to keep myself accountable, and then began to share weekly updates. What happened next was mind-blowing! Not only did I find a money-saving formula that worked for me, but my followers multiplied from 1,000 to over 158,000 (and counting) in a matter of months. It was clear it wasn't just me who needed a financial kick up the backside and it was heartening to see how many benefited from my videos, challenges, tips and thoughtful insights. It has been one of the best (and strangest) experiences of my life, but I do not take any of it for granted. Ultimately, if it was just me in my kitchen posting cash content to only ten followers, I would still continue. I am driven to do this as much for me as for anyone else.

There are always excuses and reasons not to address the overdraft elephant in the room and I have probably heard them all. Some say they don't have time to budget with cash, which tickles me as it only takes five minutes of my day. Others are keen to start but want to wait until after their holiday, Christmas or some time never. A few have even ridiculed me for my apparently old-fashioned use of cash and avoidance of contactless payments. For the most part, my budget approach has sparked an interest which has grown into a burning commitment from the many joining me on my mission. I love being part of a growing community of like-minded budget-savvy savers and spenders who unite through social media.

I want to share my strategy, along with practical advice, challenges and helpful encouragement, to give you the confidence to take control of your own finances. Whether it is with bills, food, family requirements, holidays or other responsibilities, I look at how to manage and take the pressure off this area of your life. I also share publicly, for the first time, the story of my difficult upbringing and the devastating impact this made on my relationship with money. I know some people are incredibly good at dealing with their accounts. I wasn't one of them and I am guessing you may not be either, as you are holding this book in your hands. No judgement. Welcome to my world. I think I may be able to help.

Mum Who Budgets – How It Started

I found TikTok in the first lockdown, in April 2020. I wasn't looking for anything more than an occasional escape from the relentless routine of being stuck at home. Logging on and looking through funny, thought-provoking or downright ridiculous posts was a moment of light relief from the homeschooling, remote working, repetitive cooking and endless bad news. At a point where I had very little social interaction, TikTok connected me to the outside world. I started posting my own videos, using the functions on the site to add a funny voiceover, edit a stupid dance and on one legendary occasion, perform a tribute, in a leopard-print dressing gown, to the brilliant comedienne Victoria Wood. Entertaining my family and friends became a way for me to keep my spirits up too and I knew every one of my few followers, so it was a safe space to be a clown.

I deleted the TikTok app off my phone when I found I was going to bed every night and addictively scrolling. The shift from being a welcome distraction to a vortex of lost hours was subtle, but once it felt like a habit, I knew I had to break it. Many months passed, lockdowns came and went and then, in December 2021, I was in the car with my daughter, Ava. She was messing around on her phone and decided to look at my static, cobweb-covered TikTok account. 'Mum,' she said calmly as I was trying to park, 'one of your videos has had over 100,000 views.' I thought she was mistaken. Then I thought she was winding me up. I didn't even know how to put the app back on my phone to access my feed. It turned out the video that had gone viral was one of the silliest posts of me flicking my sunglasses from the top of my head to the bridge of my nose. I just couldn't believe that so many people had found me and watched it?! I was back on TikTok.

This time around, amongst the usual random scrolling and laughing at animals doing stupid things, I came across an American woman who told the TikTok community she had saved $30,000 and paid off her debt.

As someone who has always had a difficult relationship with money (of which, more later) this caught my interest. The video was brief but life-changing. She mentioned something I had never heard of before – 'cash stuffing' – and she had a binder where she divvied out her dollars. It was so simple. I knew I had to change my spending habits; I wanted to save money, but I had no idea where to start.

I went on a scrolling frenzy, learning more about cash stuffing, which only seemed to be a thing in the USA at that time. The clever TikTok algorithm continued to push money posts in front of me. Could this be the process that pulled me back from the edge of the overdrawn hole that loomed every month? I had no option to earn more money, so I needed to be savvy with what I had coming in.

'Yes, okay, Lisa,' I hear you say at this point, 'so far, so 1970s. Who has cash these days, and what about paying my big direct-debit bills like the mortgage and electricity?' I asked those questions myself, but in light of not having solved my money issues in all the years I have been a responsible mother of three and a grandmother of two, I figured this was worth a shot. I ordered a binder without any plan of action; I just knew it would be useful once I had figured out my own approach.

The first thing I did, once my binder arrived, was to print out three random but consecutive months' bank statements as I wanted to see my pattern of spending. I steered clear of October, November and December as that would be full of Christmas costs and plumped for a more forgiving April, May and June. Armed with highlighters, I sat down and marked food bills in yellow, direct debits in pink and miscellaneous spending in green. I was deeply ashamed by the results. I was spending over £800 a month in supermarkets and, more to the point, I was throwing food away every week. So how much of that money was ending up in the bin?

Not only was I overspending in the supermarket, I was then popping into a homeware store to buy more things we didn't need. When I picked the girls up from school we would walk home past the local shop and I would buy them a sweet treat and something for dinner, even though I had plenty of food at home. It was so blinking obvious I couldn't believe I had not seen it before. I never had a shopping list, self-control or a strategy for spending, I just gravitated towards random bargains and promotions, and fooled myself into thinking I was saving money.

It sounds silly to say this now, but it was a big revelation to me. Not only had I shocked myself, I was upset at how long I had buried my head in the sand. I had not adjusted my spending habits after my third baby either. Going from a family of four to five of course impacts on the finances, but I just hadn't addressed it. It was a hard realization, but there was no denying the highlighted lines of irresponsible expense. I had nobody to blame but myself. The issue was how I was spending, against the explosive backdrop of the rising cost of living, and I needed to take fast action. Reality check, Lisa, you are the problem. But you are also the solution.

My husband Nick was cautiously optimistic about the 'new me'. He is very organized with money, so we had the occasional heated conversation about my spending habits. I would get cross and dig my heels in. I wasn't buying things for me, I would argue, I was making necessary family and home purchases, but now I could see he was right – did we really need yet another cushion? He wasn't sure I'd be able to make the leap.

The binder and the bank statements were in front of me, but I had no idea how to set a budget based on the finite monthly amount going into the account. There were also payments and direct debits that I couldn't settle by handing over a wedge of cash. Instead I took the big bills out of the planning and focused on my costs for food, petrol, birthdays and holidays.

Maybe the oddest decision I made at this point was to post a video on TikTok on 12 January 2022 of the first budget. I wanted to document the journey I was embarking on, to make myself account-able, because I knew it would stop me falling at the first hurdle. I had also been inspired by others on the platform so if just one person came across my post and was encouraged to take control of their money, then that felt like a good thing. I called myself Mum Who Budgets. Does what it says on the tin!

I did the same on the second week. I had just over 1,000 followers and I wanted to share how my baby steps in budgeting were going in case any of them were still interested. Most importantly, I didn't want to let myself down. Here was a very public way of staying on track. Over the weeks my confidence in my financial planning grew, as did my TikTok audience. When I hit 5,678 followers, I did a voiceover with a tribute to the Steps song '5, 6, 7, 8'! I couldn't quite believe how much fun I was having, on and off TikTok, by saving money.

My sister-in-law and I always joke that the 'diet starts Monday', so I thought that was a good day for money admin. I withdrew money from the cashpoint every week and returned home to stuff my binder and post a Money Monday video update. It takes a while to make this sort of financial adjustment and I didn't want to rush the new process, because I knew if I went in all guns blazing, I would probably fail. The first month was like a placebo effect where I felt in control but didn't have the proof it would work. The second month I had visual evidence in my folder that the budget was working. I could see real-life savings and I had some money left over for Nick's birthday present. By March, the third month, there were two major milestones with another birthday and a weekend away.

I didn't panic. I had budgeted for this. If I scrolled back through old TikTok videos I could see the pattern emerging.

Three months in I was getting a good response from the TikTok community and there were rolling conversations which filled my heart with hope that others were facing their money issues too. On a personal level, my visit to my binder was a positive affirmation every week. I was finally taking control and, boy, did it feel good. By April I changed from a weekly to a monthly structure. By June, TikTok featured me on FYP (For You Page, which is the first thing you see when you open the app) and my routine post got 1.7 million views with a steady stream of new followers. For the first time in five months I couldn't keep up with the comments. I think this shows how many of us are searching for a simple answer to budgeting. There were also messages from those who were negative about my approach or questioned where my money came from, suggesting I may have got cash by illegal means. Some find it so easy to be unkind on social media and type things they would never say to your face. For the few nasty comments I got, I was inundated with wonderful ones. I didn't want the content or my followers to be affected by the trolls, so I was very good at deleting anyone who wasn't there for genuine engagement in the budget conversations. I won't tolerate rudeness.

Some think this sort of exposure comes with choosing to put myself out there on a social media forum. One of the questions I am repeatedly asked, a year on, is what I do for a living and how much I earn. I totally understand why this comes up, but I also hope people accept that I wish to keep that information private. Not because I am any different from a huge proportion of the population, but because my personal circumstances aren't the point. I may mess around on a public forum and show what I have cooked for dinner, but I don't have to share everything about me. What I always say is, **focus on the method not the money** and this is the reason I have written this book and am on TikTok. I do not see myself as an influencer; the only people I want to influence are my children. The truth is, I am just me and all you get is me. Everything I do is on my terms. I find great inspiration in the TikTok community I am part of and champion others on the platform but, equally, I stick to my own way of doing things. I know it works for me.

One of the best feelings is to get responses from those I may have helped. I find it so rewarding to know that they're not going down the same bumpy and difficult road I was on several years ago. In fact, before we go forward, I would like to go back. Way back to the 1980s when I was little Lisa with a crimped fringe and home-knitted Care Bear jumper, to explain why I had such a toxic relationship with money and how I had to save myself . . .

1

Growing Up

In the Beginning

This is a hard story to tell, but an important one because it explains why my relationship with money has been so difficult. It also involves various members of my family, so I want to tread carefully, to protect them and me. This is my truth and it is the first time I have shared it publicly in the hope that it may be of some help to others. If I can build a responsible relationship with my finances, then anyone can.

Money featured a lot in my childhood, mainly because we didn't have any. My parents were very young when they had my eldest sister and then I followed exactly a year and three days later, the second of what would be four children. I knew from an early age that money was a problem, but I didn't understand why until I was older.

I have jagged memories and mixed emotions about my childhood. I remember my parents working occasionally, but most often not. Neither of them seemed to do a job for very long before they were back in the house all day, smoking and arguing. Food was a barometer of how much money we didn't have. There were times when Mum would have to scramble around for something edible and filling to feed us all. Food in the house meant there was money coming in and life would take on a brief Ready Brek glow. Dad would make Daddy Donalds (his version of McDonalds) and set up the ironing board as a counter across the kitchen door for us to order our burgers and fries from. Money meant fun too, like a big birthday party or a new paddling pool (although I found out much later that the pool was paid for by my grandparents).

I grew up observing. I was painfully aware of how little we had compared to some of my aunts, uncles and cousins, and this sparked a tiny flame of desire which burned brighter as I got older. While others holidayed abroad, we took a tent to Devon. Don't get me wrong, I know there are some people who never went away and we had the best time. I loved every moment of it. Even knowing that we couldn't afford to eat out or take part in activities unless they were free didn't ruin the joy of our no-spend holiday.

One of my defining early memories was accompanying my aunt to the supermarket and seeing how she shopped freely, without a list, just popping things she fancied into the trolley. When we got home she put the sweets and crisps into the 'treat cupboard'. A cupboard just for treats?! It was my first encounter with such a thing and it blew my mind. Not only did my aunt think this was normal, she also had drawers organized in my cousin's bedroom – one for school socks and another for recreational socks. I was lucky if I could find a pair of socks. I didn't miss a single detail of comparison. I was still very young when I realized we were poor.

Birthdays were bittersweet. My grandparents, aunts and uncles would send me cards with cash in so I could treat myself, but I never spent the money. There was a moment of excitement before it was whisked away, with Dad promising to pay me back when his giro came. He would head straight to the betting shop. I didn't know what a giro was but as far as I was concerned it never arrived. I knew it wasn't fair or right, but I was too scared to make a fuss. Nor could I tell the family members who gifted me the money and then asked what I had spent it on. I was worried that if I dared breathe a word, I would be in for it.

The only time I had money as a child was when the electricity board came to read the meter. It was an exciting day in our home. The metre was operated by inserting 50p and when it was full, or at certain times of the year, a man would come to empty the box and take what was owed to cover the usage. The rest would be given back to Mum who was always in the best of moods on these days. If there was enough, and we were lucky, she would give us each 50p, but we were sworn to secrecy. We couldn't say anything to Dad. Each time I was sure I would save mine, but I couldn't resist running to the shop at the end of our street with my siblings to buy sweets and treats. Any money I had left over would be hidden as a precaution in case Dad had a sure bet.

His gambling caused so many arguments, it stole the food from our mouths and the clothes off our backs. We very rarely watched

TV because Dad would have Teletext permanently on the screen, keeping an eye on proceedings and checking football scores, the coffee table in front of him littered with Coral gambling slips. I knew when he had money because I would come home from school and as I opened the back door I'd smell Winter Mix – sweets he bought from the market. The heady scent of clove, aniseed, eucalyptus and mint meant there would also be tins of food in the cupboard. He never came back with sweets for us though.

Even though gambling played a vital part in my childhood and influenced a lot of my memories, I knew the power it had over me would be short-lived because I was never going to make the same mistake. I have made others but I have never been tempted to gamble. I am the collateral damage.

It wasn't all doom and gloom. I had a brilliant uncle who took me and my sister away to Gran Canaria, our first trip out of the country, and a wonderful aunt who I am still in touch with now. The people I was closest to were Dad's parents, my Nan and Grandad. Little Nanny, as I called her, was short and cuddly and never made me feel any different from my better-off cousins. One wall of her lounge was a shrine to her family, covered in photographs of us all with a truly awful one of me with the crimped fringe. The memory of her makes me tearful. My grandparents didn't have favourites, we were all treated fairly, but they also did their utmost to make sure we four could fend for ourselves. She taught all her granddaughters how to cross-stitch and we each had our own sewing bag at her house. Little Nanny's devotion to us all was unquestionable and she loved nothing more than hosting big family get-togethers with her five children, their spouses and nine grandchildren. There was often a reason for a party at their house and my eyes were always on stalks at the table groaning with delicious food. As Christmas drew close, she set up a trestle table with spools of ribbon attached to one end, as a gift-wrapping station, and presented us with the most beautifully wrapped packages. She could make a box of supermarket biscuits look like there was a Gucci scarf inside!

When I went shopping with her on a Saturday, Grandad would drop us in town and she would get out her notebook where she wrote her shopping list. We would head to Littlewoods and Woolworths to get what she needed and she would never deviate from the list. It is now a tactic I swear by, and I always think of her when I write my shopping list. Both she and Grandad worked hard and tried to save money, as did most of my family. I was about seven when I realized my parents seemed to be the only ones who didn't. I remember vague bouts of employment and Mum working nights because we would have to go out in the early hours to pick her up after her shift. It was tough for her as she battled mental health issues and was eventually diagnosed bipolar when I was in my teens. Now she talks of huge regrets about the past and struggles with the guilt she feels about our childhood, but she had her own demons and reasons. I can understand how difficult it must have been for her when we were little.

When I started senior school, I got savvy. I could see how much our lack of money set us apart and I did everything I could not to stand out. Payments for school trips or discos triggered yet another argument about money and Little Nanny would often step in to cover the cost so we didn't miss out. By the time I was in my mid-teens, I learned exactly how to handle it and avoided telling my parents about any extra-curricular bills. It was easier by then as trips were optional so I just didn't go on them, which prevented a row and saved my hopes from being dashed the moment the words 'Sorry, we just can't afford it' were uttered.

Teenage Years

I felt a huge sense of responsibility to my younger siblings as I got older. I got a part-time job that quickly became three separate jobs. The first was sweeping the floor of a hairdressing salon Little Nanny would go to for her perm. The second was every Friday night in the chip shop and the third was washing up at the local sports club every Sunday. This was my first taste of financial independence and, jeez, it was good! I was fifteen, I had three incomes and I could do what I wanted. Most of all, I didn't want my younger siblings to go without like I had, and a huge proportion of my earnings went to them. I treated them as much as I could, from sweets, clothes and money for the disco to contributing towards their birthday and Christmas presents. Sometimes I would go to the supermarket across the road and buy ingredients so I could cook for everyone.

I wasn't asked or expected to do it and I didn't resent it for one moment. It felt fantastic to be able to help.

There was a walk of shame at school to get the lunch voucher, which indicated to the kitchen staff and the other pupils that the food was free. Each yellow token had a number on it which corresponded to a list which was ticked when you came to pay. They were only given to those whose parents were on government support. These sunshine-bright tokens stood out like a beacon of poverty and I refused to be stereotyped, so I would walk past the allocated collection point in the morning without collecting mine. My sister always picked hers up, she didn't care, but I would rather starve. Being poor meant you'd stand out like a giant in a crowd of ants. I was so paranoid that my friends would start whispering about me. Did they know I stitched the holes in my tights so they lasted longer? I couldn't bear the idea that people would know my parents didn't work and claimed benefits. Once I had my part-time jobs I used some of the money from my chip shop shift to pay for lunch. When friends came over to my house, I filled the cupboard and fridge with snacks so they wouldn't realize how poor we were. I was deeply ashamed.

My little brown envelope with my wages could cause the biggest of arguments. I was paid every Friday and Dad knew it. One week he said Mum had asked if she could borrow some money, so I handed the envelope over to him. On Sunday I was helping Mum with the washing and said I really fancied a fizzy drink. She said why didn't I pop to the shop and buy one as I had got paid and, without thinking, I replied that I couldn't because she had borrowed my wages. Her head spun around so fast she nearly gave herself whiplash. All hell broke out. Mum had not asked for a handout and we both knew where my wages had ended up.

My parents separated soon after that. Maybe it was the final straw, but there had been so much unhappiness and fighting over money, or rather the lack of it, over the years. It wasn't the only relationship which suffered. Our financial situation fuelled the resentment that I felt towards both my parents. My siblings and I felt we had been let down by the two people who should have done anything they could to make our lives better.

There are other reasons why my childhood was hard, but money was at the root of much of it, although I am well aware there are many people who have suffered far worse than I did. My saving grace – something I truly believe helped me be the person I am today – were the memories I clung to that sparked excitement and happiness, like my aunt's treat cupboard and her chocolate selection on the fireplace at Christmas. Little Nan's amazing spreads at every celebration, the effort she went to with present wrapping and the unconditional love she showed me. My Aunt Donna's spotless house with the peach curtains in her clean, tidy bedroom which looked like an article from an interiors magazine. All these things I wished for as a child, and I stored them away in the hope that one day I could achieve them for myself.

One of the problems with the sort of financially unstable upbringing I had was that the only talk about money was the angry, desperate, accusatory kind. We never learned about budgeting, savings, tax and pensions. Money was in one hand and out the other and there was never any planning in place. As a child, you learn how to deal with money by watching your parents and learning from them and, while I knew I could not rely on mine as role models, I wasn't sure what to do. I was earning £50 a week from my part-time jobs, which was a lot for a fifteen-year-old in the 1990s, and my guilt-free spending started. Admittedly, I was spending it on my siblings but there was no thought for the future.

After Dad left – with the TV and a lot of our furniture – things changed. There was a shift in the atmosphere in the house and the tension dropped. Both my older sister and I were working so we could contribute to the household bills and Mum's attitude towards the house changed too. She began to care about her surroundings and wanted to create a home we could be a family in. There were shopping trips and one hilarious moment when we collected an order Mum had made for what she thought was a rug at an amazing bargain price. It was tightly wrapped up but as we unravelled it, we realized the reason it was so cheap was because it was actually a doormat. We still laugh about that now.

I started college and worked at the local McDonalds – it was the best-paid job I ever had. I could work around my classes and was paid every fortnight. I just kept shopping. My sister and I walked around in faux-fur coats like we were dripping in diamonds. This was our first taste of real money and I had no idea how to behave around it so I spent it. I was aware I had to break the cycle before it broke me as it had done my parents, but I didn't expect it to happen in the way it did.

Nineteen and Pregnant

I was nineteen when I fell pregnant. I was now working in a bakery warehouse and training to be a hairdresser. I was living in a rented house, but I hadn't gone far from home as it was opposite Mum, and I could see my sister's bedroom from mine. It was ironic, because I always said I didn't want children and I certainly didn't have teen pregnancy on my vision board. It was my biggest wake-up call. Strangely, the terror I felt was not because I was embarking on single parenthood, it was the fear of financial failure for my unborn child. I worked my assets off, right up to the birth of my daughter, and I bought everything I needed. That was the first hurdle to overcome.

The second was to be able to cover all my bills and provide for my baby while I was on maternity pay. If only I had saved some money from my earlier carefree days. Did I enjoy these precious early months with Lacey, my beautiful little girl, or did I take financial responsibility and return to work? I knew it had to be the latter. I didn't want her to grow up in a struggling house as I had, with a parent who sat around moaning about being skint all the time. I found a great childminder and Mum stepped in too so I could return to work six weeks later. Whatever people's views, I knew I could hold my head high and proudly say I was providing for my child, not relying on the government.

A few months later I was made redundant, everything crashed around me and I had no choice but to accept benefits. The wheel of fortune had repeated itself. I was my parents. I scoured the papers, frantically looking for anything that would work around childcare. I was exactly who I didn't want to be. Everything I had strived to prevent was my reality and it wasn't my choice. Determined not to give up, I kept looking for work and then something good happened. I was in town buying nappies from the pound shop when I saw an advert for a new mall which was looking for employees for several stores. I had an interview with two managers and was hired on the spot. I skipped home knowing I was back in control. The only heartbreak was leaving my daughter after six months of spending every day with her. I loved being a mummy but I knew I had to break the cycle, so I took three buses every morning, dropping Lacey off at the childminder on the way before doing the return journey home and collecting her. Weekends were our time.

True Romance

This was Lacey's and my life for a couple of years until I met my now husband, Nick. When we started dating I noticed very quickly the difference in our childhood home environments. He had been exposed to a totally different upbringing, one which sounded like a dream to me. His parents both worked hard to provide for him and his sister, but they weren't spoilt kids. They spoke about happy memories, past holidays and the wonderful way they celebrated birthdays and Christmas. Every Sunday, without fail, his Mum would cook us all a roast and fuss over us. They welcomed Lacey and I with open, loving arms. They were a proper family.

Nick was brought up talking about money with his parents. They wanted their children to have the knowledge they needed for adulthood and had open discussions about savings, ISAs, mortgages and fixed rates. It was total gibberish to me but I desperately wanted to understand and learn the lingo. I still prefer an old-school approach with pen, paper and calculator though.

Lacey's relationship with Nick grew so naturally, which is testament to how special they both are. When she was three she asked if she could call him Dad, an incredible moment for all of us. He didn't even question it and immediately took on the father role. Now we were a very happy family of three. Lacey started school and Nick and I worked full time, which meant money was not an issue. It's only when I look back at this stage of life now, that I realize how much I bought my daughter's affection. I was making up for being a working parent by showering her with sweets and gifts and quietening my guilt in the process. Her birthdays and Christmas were totally over the top. I was also living vicariously through Lacey, thinking that because I never had things, she needed to have them. Except she didn't want them. The reality was that she wanted cuddles, movie nights and to help me cook dinner every now and then. When she was keen on *Hannah Montana* I made it my mission to buy any merchandise I could find. The same with *High School Musical*. When she was eight she said she didn't want a lot for her birthday, just a desk for her bedroom so she could do her homework. She was eight! This should have been an eye-opening moment for me and exactly what I needed to slow down and stop buying her everything, but I am ashamed to say I didn't see it.

I was working as a home carer at this point and then trained in palliative care. I worked three full days from 6am to 11pm, followed by five days off. At the end of my first week on the job, I woke to my first day off and the news that Mum's stepfather had been rushed to hospital. He had suffered a cardiac arrest. I went straight there and took over from Mum so she could drop my grandmother – who had early onset dementia – back home for some rest. He died peacefully while I was holding his hand. It felt like this was his gift to me, giving me experience of what was ahead in my job and showing me there was nothing to fear. I kept it together and put all my textbook training into practice. Mum came back and I sat with her while the hospital went through the bereavement protocols, and I took it all in from a professional perspective.

Being a domiciliary care worker was the most rewarding job I have ever had. When I told people what I did they would say, ' Oh, so you wipe arses for a living and give Doris her medication?' or the worst, ' You're just a carer.' Just. It felt anything but and so dismissive to me. It was an utter privilege to look after people who needed specialist help or were at the end of their lives. On my days off I would worry about those under my care and once, when it snowed, Lacey and I walked to one lady's house to check she was okay.

Working in the health and social care sector meant that some weeks I could be earning £700 and others my wages would amount to £300, but it was more than enough to pay bills and splurge on a few little luxuries. However, I was living from pay cheque to pay cheque with no thought of saving anything. Now I had another spending excuse because Nick and I were planning our wedding. Then I became pregnant with our second daughter Ava, and this should have been my financial wake-up call as I was going to have to survive on maternity pay. Nick pointed out the nice little overdraft I was racking up as I was still spending money like I was earning it. It was a massive shock to the system and took me straight back to those early days of Lacey's childhood. I had to try and keep it in check until I could return to work and a proper salary. Luckily for me, Nick could help out financially so the combination of me cutting back and him supporting me meant I didn't get into serious money trouble. It was very different from my first experience.

By the time I was pregnant with our third daughter Poppy it

was clear that I could not stay in full-time employment, as most of my money would be going on childcare. Nick was working all hours to build his business, so it made sense for me to take a step back and find a part-time job which worked around the family. It was the right thing for us then and it still is now.

While all this made sense, I didn't feel I was contributing financially like I should. It wasn't about earning more money, because that wasn't possible. It was about being clever with what I had. I wanted to feel validated when I bought Nick presents, knowing it was coming from me not our joint bank account. Nick never complained about money and we both loved the fact I was at home more and could spend valuable time with my girls, something I regretted missing out on with Lacey. It was time versus money and time won, but money can't be ignored. So, when I was aimlessly scrolling through TikTok at the end of 2021 and came across a woman solving her debt problems, my attention was caught.

I was subconsciously looking for help. I didn't know it at the time, but my toxic attitude to money against the backdrop of my upbringing and the compulsion to spend anything I earned were catching up with me. I was unsettled by my finances and the fear that history might repeat itself. Seeing someone on social media able to completely reverse their spending habits, learn how to save and pay off their debts was like a big neon sign flashing 'come this way'. It felt like she was put there for me at exactly the moment I needed her. Maybe my story and my approach to budgeting could trigger the same shift in you too? It is all about having a money mindset.

2

Money Mindset

It's funny how most of us feel we are in control of our money because we are the ones that spend it. I was totally hoodwinked by this. I thought if I didn't lose my bank cards or share my pin number and checked my bank statements regularly then I was practising good money management. What I didn't do was look at my behaviour around money, how much I spent and consider what changes could be made. Had I done so I would have realized that I was massively overspending in one area and ignoring all the others. My mindset around money was denial, awkwardness, bravado and to hope for the best while keeping my fingers permanently crossed. Sound familiar?!

Money is still a taboo subject in modern society. How we talk – or more importantly do not talk – about our finances is fascinating, considering all the other things we are so open about these days. Historically, if you were British, it was considered ill-mannered and rude to talk about money, and this seems to have stuck fast. People are embarrassed to reveal anything about their financial situation, so they often lie, embellish, clam up or joke about it instead. The judgement around being too poor or too rich, living in council accommodation or a huge house, visiting food banks or ordering online upmarket food deliveries, is powerful and pervasive. Better then to avoid the topic completely. Can't pay your rent? Terrible credit rating? Letter from the bailiffs? Move along, nothing to see here.

I understand, I've been there. But these are all issues we need to be more vocal about, as well as sharing our experiences, giving advice and finding ways to have comfortable conversations around financial matters. Now more than ever. Each and every one of us is affected by national and global economic crises. We live against the backdrop of rising inflation, recession, union strikes and a cost-of-living crisis. Each new government budget brings its own personal fears, so we need to be more prepared and ready for an ever-changing world. Budgeting is a fundamental weapon to use in our financial battle.

There seems to be little importance placed on the impact money has on us, nor is there a clear structure of support in place to educate people on financial management. Our society encourages a healthy attitude to life through eating, exercising and good mental health, so why is a healthy relationship with money not on this list too? Instead we are bombarded by billboards, TV advertising and print media telling us to buy things, because if we do we will be complete. We will be happy. We are influenced by the opinions and judgements of others, seduced by lifestyles and celebrity-endorsed brands we see on social media. The call to consumerism is often too seductive to ignore.

We are also a culture of convenience. We can purchase almost anything we want at the touch of a button or a quick-tap transaction. Forgot your card? Don't worry, pay for it with your phone! Came out without your phone? Not a problem, use your watch! What was once a simple 'pay as you go' has been replaced with credit cards, contactless, chip and pin, Paypal, online purchasing and the lure of zero-percent interest. This robotic approach doesn't even feel like money and the deficit it makes in our account barely registers in our brain. As long as the payment is approved we can breathe an inward sigh of relief and get on with our day. We are so conditioned not to use cash any more that cashiers often assume I will pay by card and are almost indignant when I don't, particularly in the supermarket. There is generally a bit of tutting and head shaking and I feel like a curious circus oddity. It should be acceptable to pay for things with real money and yet we have been thrust into a cashless society where we rely on cards, online orders and home deliveries.

I find it interesting that we think nothing of buying a mobile phone, sofa or telly and signing ourselves up to two years of debt, rather than taking the alternative view and saving the money before we spend it. Quick-fix options are not the answer. A credit card, interest-free finance and an overdraft may help in the short term, but unless you have a clear plan to pay them off, they will ultimately add to the financial burden. We may convince ourselves that these are extenuating circumstances and we won't have the same problem again, but what if another issue comes along? And then another? The snowball effect picks up speed and before we know it, we are completely out of our depth. We live in disorganized chaos, which we gloomily refer to as 'the cost of living' or, if there is something we don't want to miss out on we justify it with a jolly 'you only live once!'

As I dug deeper, trying to understand why my relationship with money was unhealthy for so long, I could see how many others had the same issues, whether they had been brought up in an environment like mine or not. The thing that seems to connect us all is the lack of understanding about money, budgeting and saving from an early age. I look at the younger generation now and they have no concept of what things cost. I showed my daughter, Ava, the end result of my savings challenge. She was shocked to see how many weeks it had taken me to save up and it was her first lesson in physically moving money around. How can a young person truly understand the value of something if it's just digits on a screen? How can they understand it if they are not taught how? I've come to realize it is very much a learned knowledge, which brings me to one of my big bugbears: financial education in school. Or the lack of it.

Why don't schools educate children on how to budget, save and spend money? We cannot assume that these sorts of life skills will be taught at home. Surely this is as beneficial as other maths subjects like trigonometry and algebra and is about teaching children independence with the ability to function in the real world. Clearly, I am not a teacher, but I think there is a massive kink in the education system when it comes to preparing the next generation for their financial future. Understanding money is a vital part of human development.

The Money and Pensions Service publishes financial education guidance for schools and hosts a Talk Money Week, running events and activities around the UK encouraging all of us to chat about money – from pocket money to pensions. They suggest that the ages of four to seven are a great time to tackle the basics, and that seven to eleven-year-olds can be taught responsibility, with pocket money being a good tool. They then go on to say that eleven to eighteen is the key age bracket to teach financial responsibilities and prepare for adulthood. Not being exposed to this knowledge could result in poor credit, borrowing, financial debt and mental health issues.

Not only should schools get involved but parents must also take responsibility for educating their children. That said, we need to find the right balance when talking to our children about money. They should not be subject to any financial stress we may be under, exposed to the harsh realities or told the complete truth. This is about giving them a general understanding of money and a respect for their finances, not sharing our woes. I am on a mission to raise awareness around this important issue as loudly as I can bang my budget drum. I often think about those children growing up in a similar environment to me and the little knowledge they will have on this subject. They will only see the bad side of money.

A lack of budgeting is like standing on a trap door, with all our excuses shoved underneath us, while we anxiously hope the door will not give way, sending us plummeting into the murky abyss. Open it now and deal with it on your own terms, before it is too late. I see so many who refuse to live within their means. Ultimately, the stress this puts them under is not worth the hedonistic, devil-may-care front they hide behind. Money worries can impact every area of our lives. I was one of those people who was 'bad with money'. I equated money with happiness and whenever I felt low, I would pop to the shops to purchase something for my children. It was a temporary fix. I would be cheered up in the short term, but it wasn't the solution, it just stuck a band aid over the problem for a while. Now I operate within a budget, my mental health has benefited as well as my bank balance. The control I have over my finances has made me feel more in charge in other areas of my life and I no longer feel like I am **riding the rollercoaster of credit**. Or waiting for an unwelcome surprise.

What if you focused on budgeting with the real money you have rather than relying on cards and online purchasing? Using cash instead may sound like an old-fashioned way of buying things, but you can physically see it leaving your purse and that makes you think twice before spending it. It's not about stepping back in time to the days of paying half a shilling for a bag of peppermints, it's about leaping forward with all the knowledge at your fingertips and choosing what works for you. In today's world, it is impossible not to use direct debits and online payments, but it doesn't have to be for everything you owe.

Incorporating coins and notes into my routine stays in my memory in a way card payments do not. I don't forget how much my weekly shop was when I have to physically take the money from my purse to pay for it, and I also remember what I have left to spend. Before the binder and the method, I would have to check my online banking app and there were times when I couldn't bring myself to look and see what the damage was. And damage is the right word for it.

The first thing to overcome is a defeatist attitude. So many people say to me they are stuck in a cycle of minimum earnings and maximum outgoings. There is no spare money to save, they say, almost accusing me of hiding a secret pot of cash or expecting me to wave a magic wand. Of course, there are people – too many of them – who find it impossible to pay for the fundamentals in life, let alone think about the extras like birthday presents or a day trip. But there are also those, me included, who make it harder for ourselves than it needs to be. There is no point making assumptions about what your financial position is, you need to know what you are dealing with and, in turn, make sure you are prepared for the twists and turns of our capitalist society.

The truth about creating a budget is that it doesn't change what you already have, it just makes it work smarter and harder for you. It's not that your bank account has been lying to you all this time and you have just found out it is not a bottomless well, it is what it is. After the initial shock of this you really can take control. The hardest part of creating a budget for yourself is looking at that bank account statement and realizing where it went wrong, areas of overspending and most importantly knowing it can be turned around and you will find success with your finances. As you buy things, ask yourself, do you NEED it or do you WANT it? If it is the former then go ahead, if it is the latter then stop. Distract yourself. Clean the fridge, watch TV, call a friend. Now ask yourself again, do you still want it? The chances are the frisson of excitement and the urge has passed.

Not only have I managed to positively change my money mindset, but I have seen the evidence in my bank account. The truth is, I hated money and the problems that came with not having it and then having it. Now it is something I am proud of managing. I HAVE TAKEN BACK CONTROL! I am living proof that budgeting doesn't mean cheap short cuts and restrictions. The excitement of spending has now flipped to the excitement of saving and I want to take you on the journey too. It's time to give the budget a happy makeover!

Why Cash Matters

Before I take you (hopefully not kicking and screaming) into the wonderful world of budgeting, I wanted to make a point about saving and spending real money in case you still need convincing. This is one of my favourite subjects so excuse me while I climb up on to my soap box. Cash is important. The less we use it the more likely we are to lose it and there are three crucial reasons why we shouldn't let this happen: our privacy, our power and our freedom. I know this may sound dramatic – and highly unlikely you may think – but look how easy it is to pay for things without money.

We are now so used to direct debits, bank transfers, contactless and online purchases that I wonder when was the last time you held a crisp ten-pound note in your hand? There used to be queues at the cashpoint to get money out, but now many high street banks and holes in the wall are closing. Neither is it illegal for shops to reject cash payments. Nobody seems to need real money these days and the wheels are already in motion for further alternative banking. There have been discussions between the Government and the Bank of England about a new form of digital, non-physical currency – central bank digital currency (CBDC). Whatever the potential gains of this system for us, the people, it makes me question the lack of security, personal control and autonomy I would have within it and how much would be taken over by a centralized system. Like living in a digital Big Brother simulation where our money only exists as numbers on a screen, every transaction can be traced, data used and judgements made. Not to mention the margin for technical errors. Can you imagine if you are doing your weekly shop and suddenly the computer says 'NO'?! Or you fill the car with petrol and find the system is down, again?!

I find these possible developments frightening, particularly as budgeting with coins and notes has saved me from a toxic financial past. Without cash stuffing, it is likely I would still be struggling from one month to the next and pretending I wasn't. Relinquishing responsibility for our money is exactly when we get into trouble with it. Just because technology and society are moving on does not mean that cash cannot be part of our future too. So, when I rant about saving and paying for certain things with actual money, or risk not having the option in the future, I really mean it.

I will share with you how it all works. But first, let's take a closer look at some different approaches to money. I find them best explained when they take the guise of characters, so that you can understand which one matches your personality.

Cash Characters

The Peacock

It's all for show. The Peacock loves to boast about their successful achievements and enviable riches, but how much of it is true? With a 'money no object' attitude and a lot of fanciful parading and preening, you can't begin to imagine their wealth. But then again neither can they, as it is all in their lurid imagination. Beneath the feathered display is the complicated chaos of overdrafts, credit cards and loans that they are staying just one tenuous step ahead of. Beware, one day a peacock, the next day a pigeon.

The Keep-Ups

Keeping up with the Joneses is an easy trap to fall into. The Keep-Ups are part of a social group that controls the tone of their spending. Every purchase is influenced by their friends – like a car, holiday and outfits – but without the same healthy bank balance. The Keep-Ups constantly strive to stay in the gang, risking debt rather than the cold shoulder. They may even have to go one step further, buying bigger and better than their dear pals to prevent anyone suspecting they are out of their depth. If only the Keep-Ups could become the Enlightened and save themselves before it is too late. Those friends are not worth getting into financial trouble over and they certainly won't pay off the overdraft.

The Glory Hunter

Eaten away by envy, the Glory Hunter just cannot understand how others can afford things that they are not able to. Whether it's a vacation, a new pair of trainers or a kitchen extension, they want to know how on earth others have managed to pay for it?! They do not consider the hard-working journey to get there, they just focus on the moment of glory. They assume others are keeping quiet about winning the lottery, claiming an inheritance or just lying about their job. The Glory Hunters are consumed by other people's good news and refuse to accept that genuine hard graft and careful saving plays a vital part in others' success. This is a dangerous trait to have around money as it can easily cloud judgement and affect attitudes. Look straight ahead and do not be distracted by seemingly more successful peers. After all, they could be Peacocks!

The Serious Saver

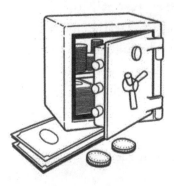

These are the gifted amongst us, those with a natural financial ability and healthy respect for money. They save for a rainy day, have a pension plan, live within their means and enjoy budgeting. There are no rash moves or bad credit ratings and they are NEVER in overdraft. Sometimes the Serious Saver is called Scrooge, as they can tip into frugality and ignore the lure of pointless promotions or quick-decision purchases. Their mantra is to count the pennies and the pounds will look after themselves. Not to be mistaken for the Tight Ass.

The Tight Ass

Otherwise known as the Penny Pincher, the Tight-Ass never knowingly overspends on anything. At the end of a meal out – if they can even cope with being in a restaurant – they use their mathematical wizardry skills to work out what they owe. Just in case the establishment, or even their friends, are trying to swindle them. Parting with money is a painful process, down to the last penny. They scrutinize the till receipt at the supermarket and always remember whose turn it is to buy coffee. The TA thinks nothing of re-gifting to save themselves a buck and they wear their shoes until they are falling apart (and even then, they will attempt to glue them back together to get another week's wear). Interestingly, their relationship with money can be fragile and they risk relationships over it. Others avoid any financial links with these people as borrowing a fiver will be at the forefront of their mind until it is paid back.

The Borrower

Oh, woe is the Borrower and their repetitive cycle of spend, borrow and spend again. They have no concept of good money management or an idea of how to get themselves out of the financial black hole they have fallen into. Their income is overstretched to the point of bursting and they go for short-term solutions without considering future issues. The Borrower is in a difficult pattern of behaviour, relying on others to help, whether they are family, friends or the bank. At some point their luck may run out, as those who support them grow tired of giving handouts.

The Ostrich

Many of us have been the Ostrich at some point in our lives. Preferring to remain in denial about their finances, the Ostrich buries their head in the sand and hopes for divine financial intervention. They are not hopeless with money, but they aren't brilliant either. They hold their breath when using their bank card, forget to check their statements and are convinced that next month will be better. Occasionally, the Ostrich will lift their head up and take enough notice to arrange a mortgage, set up a pension or pay off their overdraft. Which takes them by surprise and lulls them into a false sense of being the Serious Saver. They are not, but they may just be able to take control.

The Eye-Opener

The Eye-Opener had a revelation when they realized their spending habits had reached a critical point and if they didn't act then the next stop is debtor's prison and gruel for dinner. They may have been a Peacock, an Ostrich or a Borrower, but now the mask they once wore has slipped and all that is left is the painful truth of their situation. Fear is replaced by acceptance followed by excitement at the new possibilities surrounding their relationship with money. There is no overnight fix, but they are ready to admit their mistakes and work on themselves to make the changes needed. The Eye-Opener becomes the Serious Saver! This is me by the way. Although you have probably already gathered that . . .

3

The Budgeting Method

The hardest part of the budgeting exercise was accepting that it was me who had to change. It is so easy to point the finger of blame at something or someone else. I didn't want to believe I had got myself into such a mess, or that I was the only one who could get myself out of it. I know many people can relate to this and they struggle with the realization that alterations need to be made – in their lifestyles, spending, income and attitude. For some, a budget has a terrible reputation. It's BORING, people moan, as they beep their card for yet another contactless transaction. Who has time to go through bank statements and plan the month ahead, they yawn. But budgets don't have to be boring or restrictive. It's not about depriving ourselves, it is about driving what money we have into the areas that require it most, using foresight, organization and patience. You owe it to yourself to be honest.

My budget success is based on cash stuffing and is a personal endeavour I am incredibly proud of. However, I am very aware that everyone's financial and domestic situations are different. It works for me to be the lone ranger on this part of my money journey, but you may prefer to share the process and the binder with your partner, flatmate or the rest of your family. Or buy them their own binders so you can each run your savings challenges and compare notes. There is nothing like a bit of healthy competition to keep focused! Whichever way you choose to tackle this, just think of me as your cheerleader, with pom poms and a few high kicks. Although I won't be doing the splits, as I am not sure I could get up again.

So, what are you waiting for?!

Life without a budget can mean:

STRESS

DOWNWARD SPIRAL OF BORROWING

OVERDRAFT

MOUNTING DEBT

ANXIETY

OVERSPENDING

ARGUMENTS

DELUSION

Life with a budget can mean:

FACING REALITY

BEING ORGANISED + REWARDED

SIMPLIFIES LIFE DECISIONS

MEETING EXPECTATIONS

CLEAR KNOWLEDGE of FINANCES

CONTROL + POWER

HAVING FUN!

Let's Get Started

The first step is to look at your bank statements. Not just a cursory glance online to check for fraudulent activity or to see if a fairy godmother has popped a few hundred pounds into your account. I hate to break it to you, but that is unlikely to happen. I would recommend physically printing out several consecutive months of statements which include all standing orders and direct debits. As you know, I chose to pick a quieter period of the year rather than the one leading up to Christmas, to give me a clear understanding of general costs. Grab a few different coloured highlighters, a pen and a notebook, and start to group your bills so you can get a good idea of where your money is going. I marked food shopping, homewares, direct debits and miscellaneous in different colours, and I could see instantly what the main problem was for me: the supermarket.

Make a list of:

Fundamentals (**anything that is paid by direct debit**) *like* . . .

- Mortgage/rent
- Utilities
- Insurances
- Pension
- Childcare
- Loan repayments/credit cards
- Memberships

Add these costs up to find the total amount you need in your bank every month to cover these outgoings. Take the figure off your monthly income. What you have left is what will pay for:

Necessities like . . .

- Food
- Petrol
- Bills that you don't pay by direct debit – e.g. water, car insurance
- Home maintenance
- Clothes
- School trips
- Any additionals

The final list of monthly costs could include:

Recreational like . . .

- Birthdays
- Christmas
- Festivals/celebrations
- Events
- Holidays
- Clubs
- Hobbies

So, now you have a good picture of where your money goes, but how do you set a budget and implement it practically? Here is the first part of a savings and cash stuffing structure that I use. There is more to share with you in future pages, but for now begin slowly and don't over-complicate matters, because then you are more likely to stick to the budget plan. I would suggest picking two or three savings categories from your necessities and recreational lists that you want to focus on so you are not overwhelmed; for example, food, petrol and Christmas. As your confidence grows you can incorporate more categories into your binder.

- Go through your highlighted statements. Can you reduce or delete any of your payments? At this point, I could see how much I was spending at the supermarket and knew I would be able to significantly cut my spending there. I also looked at any direct debits that could be cancelled. Do you have a rogue gym membership, insurance you aren't sure why you pay or a satellite network you never watch? Make sure every payment is interrogated and found to be important. This budget works because it is about **making the most out of what you already have.**

- Work out the total cost of all your direct debits and take this away from your income. The figure you have left needs to cover all your necessities and recreational costs, and leave a small amount in your bank for emergencies.

- Decide which categories you are going to include in your cash stuffing exercise and how much money you can assign to each.

- Withdraw the cash amount.

- Yes, you heard me. Once you are in the swing of this, any bills and other payments which can be paid for in actual, real money should be.

- Using the binder or envelopes, divide the cash between each of your chosen categories.

- When you buy food or petrol, remember to take the money with you and keep within your budget, buying what you can afford rather than using your bank card to make up any shortfall.

- Repeat this process the following week.

- And the week after that.

This is a great start. Do not feel you need to rush on to the next stage immediately. It is more important to get comfortable with the idea of budgeting and cash stuffing in specific areas of your life before you move on.

Why a Binder?

When I came across that American lady posting about clearing her $30,000 debt on TikTok, it wasn't her achievement that stuck with me – as praiseworthy as that was – it was her binder. What caught my attention was the method, not the money, and it percolated away in the far, dusty recesses of my brain. This woman used a binder to separate her money and keep her expenses in check. She SAVED every week until her debt was clear. It was so simple and effective that I kept thinking about what I could do if only I had a binder. A quick search online showed 'money saving binders' in multiple colours, so I bought a pink one because, you know, PINK!

Once I had worked out which things I was going to save for, I labelled the plastic pouches in the binder in readiness for my first cash stuffing. As well as food, I included day trips, date night, Nick's birthday, Christmas, home décor and school. I figured if this couldn't stop my spontaneous spending then I am not sure what would. As my new budget plan progressed, I became more comfortable with the process and could see it was working. Time to take it up a level and, *voilà*, I bought a second binder to focus solely on everyone's birthdays, then a third for holidays. I am now a three binder kinda gal.

My most asked question is where I got my binders from. I do include a link on my TikTok bio but they are easy to find online. If you would prefer not to spend the money then use paper envelopes instead and store them safely in a plastic folder. I know there are various different methods that people use, but I don't get swayed because the binder works for me. I do tuck mine away in a secret place (which I shall never reveal!) and it is good to keep it out of my sight line too.

The Next Stage

Once you are comfortable with the weekly process and you can see it is working, you could move on to a monthly routine for everything apart from food, which is easier to keep as a weekly withdrawal. This change in approach won't suit everyone because it depends when you are paid, but it works for me as my income and direct debits hit my account monthly. If you are now familiar with stashing some cash for the basic necessities, like food and petrol, you can consider tackling the other areas of your finances.

Decide which categories are important to you (for inspiration, go to the section Cash Stuffing Categories on page 64) and label your binder accordingly. Then crack on with the next level of the process:

- To help you remain on track, there are two key dates to note in your calendar. The first is Money Admin Day – this is the day I add money into my binder. I choose to do this on the first of the month as it ties in with my payments and debits. The second is Money Stocktake Day, where I make a budget plan for the next month midway through the current month.

- Money Stocktake Day is a halfway check point, when you consult your calendar and banking app to look at the month ahead. Make a note of your income and direct debits for the following month. This will help you plan a budget with what you have left and assign a proportion of that to each of your envelopes, whatever they are for. Do a stocktake of your social calendar too, looking at upcoming events to ensure you have the funds available to keep in line with your budget. This is a crucial way of navigating through any financial surprises like rising energy and food bills.

- Write this plan down so when Money Admin Day comes around you know exactly what you are doing. This is about preparing ahead of time.

- On Money Admin Day, the first of the month, draw out the cash you need and replenish your binder. Divide it between your chosen categories, using the plan you devised on Money Stocktake Day.

- The only money you need to continue to draw out weekly is for food, so you need to leave enough in your account to cover this throughout the month. I budget £90 a week, which I withdraw every Monday, so I work out whether the month has four or five Mondays.

- Remember not to clear out your account. You need to leave some money in there in case of nice, or not so nice, surprises.

- It can be tricky to work out how much to save for certain outgoings and some are annual events, which don't always need a monthly input or demand a set amount. Set targets for yourself. For example, if you want to save £500 for Christmas, then work out whether you will spread the cost across six months at around £83 a month or a more palatable monthly instalment of £42 over a year. Or you may want to spend the first half of the year saving £83 a month for a holiday before switching to Christmas for the second half. I knew I needed a solid plan for annual events, because this is one of the areas where I would come unstuck with overspending. It is important to have a goal but the amount you assign to this is totally up to you. Do not be unrealistic. If you do not have the income to support a large savings plan, either take longer to save up or reduce the final amount you would wish for. Saving something is better than nothing.

- Do not get carried away and overstuff your envelopes, only to discover you have run out of money halfway through the month.

- Do not spread your money out thinly across many different categories. The cash you have needs to make the biggest, most useful impact.

- One of the big issues we face is a rising cost in living. This can destabilize even the best-organized budgeter as they watch their household bills increase. Adjusting your budget accordingly may mean taking out less cash each month or reducing payments in recreational pots. The process of budgeting is exactly that, a process. It continues to shift and we need to be ahead of it, to make our money work for us. Heading towards winter means more money on heating bills and in the spring this can be adjusted accordingly for the summer. If you deal with it before it happens, the chances are you will be able to avoid some of the anxiety and panic attached to rising costs.

Lisa's Cash Stuffing Case Study

I hope you are not feeling too bamboozled by everything I have shared so far. One of the best ways to understand the process is to see it in action. As I do on TikTok, I thought it would be useful to take you through my Money Stocktake Day and Money Admin Day, to help you make your budget plan a reality. Come and join me in my kitchen, where the kettle is on for coffee and the distant whirring sound you can hear is my hard-working washing machine. Ignore the dog. Are you sitting comfortably? Right, let's begin . . .

Money Stocktake Day

Believe me when I tell you a regular stocktake of your accounts is a quick and easy way to check your finances, one that does not require countless hours of number crunching. Simple yet rewarding is my motto. I do this midway through the month to help me stay on track with my bank activity and help me prepare for next month's budgeting figures. It is equally as important as the monthly Money Admin Day, because without it I could end up back where I started and that is not a risk I am willing to take. One of the main advantages of doing a fortnightly stocktake of my finances is that it helps me understand my spending behaviour and enables me to remain focused and on track. I also find this process super exciting. I know, saying budgeting and exciting in the same sentence may seem weird, but just trust the process and you will reap the benefits. Everything I do to pre-plan and implement my budget is for the sole purpose of giving me back control of my money.

I am a basic budgeter so no laptop, online money app or complicated spreadsheets. These are the tools I use:

- Notebook and pen
- Calculator.
- Online bank statement
- Calendar
- A cuppa

Armed with my notebook, I write down both mine and Nick's incomes. We have a set amount coming in each month, so our figures do not change. If yours do, then you will need to adjust your budget each time to stay in line with what you are earning – reducing or boosting your cash stuffing accordingly.

I go online to check all upcoming direct debits. For us, our bills are set to come out before the 10th of each month. I add all the direct debits together and record the figure on the page.

The next is food, based on the number of Mondays I have in that month. At a set amount of £90 a week, I will either need £360 or £450 so I leave that in the bank and withdraw it weekly for my food shop.

Once I have written down my income, direct debits and food costs I go to my binder.

Now I list every single category which is active in my binder and make a note of the amounts I hope to put into it.

I add those amounts up and deduct the binder total from my remaining income. If the numbers don't tally, I will tweak them in line with what I can afford to contribute that month.

Then I confirm the amounts. I note down exactly what I would like to put in each of the envelopes in my binders. The food and binder amounts are also deducted from the overall income.

At this point I have a clear picture of what is ahead and the reassurance that I have assigned my budget to cover all possibilities. I say all, but I am well aware there could be something lurking that will catch me out, which is why I leave any remaining money in the bank. It's good to have a contingency for an unforeseen emergency like the boiler breaking down, or for any upcoming special events.

I always check the calendar to see what is planned, whether it's birthdays, parties or trips with friends. It is important to know what is ahead so there are no financial surprises, like a train ticket I didn't account for or a drinks bill at the pub. I try my best each month not to touch this, but if I have to I don't get hung up over it as I know all the important things in our life are accounted for.

Money Admin Day

Money Admin Day is always the first of the month. It is the day I stuff my binder envelopes with cash referring to the plan I have drawn up on Money Stocktake Day. As I have said, this may not work for you as it depends when you are paid, but I would still recommend a monthly overview. A couple of days before the first of the month, I double check my figures and refer to the list so I know exactly what is going into my binder that month and draw out the total amount from the local ATM, Post Office or bank. If I go to the bank, I make sure the trek into town is beneficial in other ways so I can combine a few chores in one trip. I often avoid using a cashpoint if I need a variety of notes – I may need five £5 notes for example – so withdrawing money from a real person is the best option.

Back at home, with my coffee, cash and binders, I am ready to start my money admin process. Checking the list I have written on Money Stocktake Day, I know precisely how much I need to put in each of my envelopes. In the first binder is:

Petrol	£60
Socializing	£50
Window cleaning	£14
Water bill	£35
Car insurance	£30
Just-in-case fund	£50
School trips	£20–£40

My second binder is for the purpose of saving for birthday presents and I follow the same process as the first, cross referencing with my list to ensure my maths matches the amounts I can put away. Each envelope is titled as below:

Gifts (*for my children to take to friends' birthday parties*)	£10
Lacey	£15
Ava	£20
Poppy	£20
Nick	£30
Other family members	£20
Grandchildren	£20

My third binder is seasonal and covers holidays – and I can't promise I will stop there. I have a fourth lined up for Christmas and who knows what else will need its own binder in the future. Once you top up, you just can't stop. After I have allocated all the cash, I close my binders and put them away safely. I resist any temptation to move money around again or deviate from the plan I have put together. Roll on the next stocktake two weeks later.

So, now you have an idea of how my financial planning works, here are two more case studies of anonymous folk who shared their figures with me. I think it is really useful to see how others tackle their budget before you focus on your own.

Case Study - Single Person

Income	£1650
Monthly outgoings:	
Rent including bills	£450
Food	£150
Transport	£70
Phone and subscriptions	£65
Total	£735
Binder:	
Eating out/entertainment	£150
Misc	£100
Savings to cover birthdays, Christmas, holiday	£200
Pension	£100
Remaining in the bank	£365

Case Study - Couple with Joint Income

Income	£2500

Outgoings:

Mortgage	£805
Household bills	£200
Phone	£30
Insurance	£30
Water bill	£35
Internet/broadband	£30

Total	£1,130

Binder:

Food shop	£200
Eating out	£100
Socializing	£100
Petrol	£100
Savings	£150
Christmas	£80
Birthday	£40

Remaining in the bank	£600

4

Cash Stuffing Categories

My cash stuffing categories reflect my life and needs. They are the significant savings I want to make once my fundamental bills have been paid. Yours are likely to be different, although there are several which are universal for many of us. I can't make this decision for you or recommend you copy me entirely, as your plan needs to be bespoke for your requirements. What I will say is the categories which have worked best for me, other than food, petrol and birthdays, are my socializing and savings envelopes, which have been very handy for the occasional takeaway and manicure. I also call these my sinking funds, amounts that I put away monthly that aren't for the crucial bills. They are included in my binder to prevent me from using my cards as frequently as I used to.

I think this is one of the biggest points to make in my cash-not-card mission. It is about creating a system which is designed to limit (not eradicate) your card use and help you navigate through those moments when you are most likely to get caught out. Like a coffee shop stop-off, a spontaneous clothes shopping trip or being trapped in a Five Guys burger joint in a hurricane . . . No?! Just me that wishes that would happen then?! Take your saved cash not your card with you for any of these eventualities. Who wants to slip up when you are feeling in control and there are hopeful signs of green shoots in your desert of a bank account?

To help you put your binder together, I have looked at the central categories that may become part of your budget planning and given some good, solid advice, learned the hard way!

The Food Shop

- **Face facts:** How much are you spending on food each week? What are your requirements based on the number of people you are feeding as well as dietary and allergy requirements (as these could make your shop more expensive)? I spent many years dismissing my spending as just 'the cost of normal everyday life' and that 'my family has to eat.' Unsurprisingly, when I went through my bank statements the biggest repeated expenditure was the supermarket shop. The truth was only a proportion of the money was spent on food for the family, the rest disappeared on clothing, homeware, special deals or another bargain in the supermarket I didn't need. I knew I could reduce it. I had to stop the daily trips to the local shop for 'a few bits' and I needed to drastically cut the supermarket bill.

- **Waste not, want not:** I was throwing money away each week. This was either because I had not checked the shelf life of products or because of my choices were inspired by wonderful merchandising campaigns, discount labels and offers. Every week I was unmotivated to work out what to cook as I never seemed to have all the right ingredients for a particular meal. How could I have bought all those things and not be able to conjure up dinner? Instead I wrote a list each week and I did not rush the shopping, but gave myself time to check dates and labels as I went around the aisles. It may sound obvious to say this, but don't forget to pick items with the longest shelf life. Or the items that are reduced because they are out of date, but could fit in your freezer.

- **No list, no hope:** Everything changed when I started menu planning. At the beginning of the week, I write down seven meals to cook. Then I check the fridge and cupboards in case I already have some of the ingredients and can cross them off my list. In my weekly budget, I buy stuff for breakfast, packed lunches, dinner, snacks, pet food, personal care and cleaning products (but it does not include alcohol). I take the list with me to the shops and I stick to it. Yep, it's that easy. Only buy what you need and this will help you stay in budget. It is unlikely that anyone will starve. In the first month I used this approach, I was really strict because I was trying to use up things I had from previous bulk buys and tailored the menu accordingly. None of my family noticed! (Check out the example of my supermarket shopping list on page 71.)

- **Hero ingredients:** Look at the staple produce you use every week that can work in multiple recipes. For example, I often buy peppers which can be used in a pasta bake, chicken fajitas and a stir fry.

- **Family favourites**: Talk to those you cook for to check what they like and avoid spending more money cooking different things to keep everyone happy. That's not to say that you have to stick to the same dishes week in, week out, you can try new things too, but it helps to have a structure when you budget. We have a treat cupboard too but now it only has a week's worth of snacks rather than looking like the inside of Willy Wonka's factory!

- **Stay focused**: I would dash from store to store to purchase cleaning products, homeware, beauty products and snacks. It was like I was a contestant in my own *Supermarket Sweep*, picking up everything apart from the giant inflatable banana and without Dale Winton encouraging me from the aisles. I told myself I was in search of the best deals, so it was worth zooming around several different shops. The truth was I had more temptation to deviate from what I was supposed to be buying so I would always come out with more than I needed. Sometimes it is cheaper to do all your shopping in one place, even if it means spending a few pence more on an item.

- **Bulk buy dilemma**: Buying in bulk only makes budget sense if you do it monthly. I was doing it weekly, so you can imagine . . .

- **Bring bags**: My car boot was overflowing with shopping bags. I would forget to take them in with me and then purchase more at the checkout. The Bag for Life was more like the bag for a week for me as I just added them to the collection I already had – and they were often the more expensive woven totes rather than the plastic bags. If I added up the number of bags I have bought I bet it would be enough to pay for me to have my hair done, twice.

- **The psychology of the store:** Every now and again you may find your supermarket shifts sections around which confuses your well-trodden path to your usual purchases. This means you will be distracted by new things as you try to do your weekly shop. Do not succumb! I always say exploring equals expense.

- **Small is better:** Whichever supermarket you choose to shop in, do not always go into the biggest version of it as they are a minefield of overwhelming options. Stick to the smaller stores for your weekly shop so you are not tempted by the clothing, homeware and electronics sections. Also consider size when choosing your trolley. Go for the smaller version as it is all too easy to fill a big trolley with stuff you don't need but can't resist. For the same reason, if you only have a few items to get, pick up a basket instead.

- **Don't spend it all at once:** I only take two thirds of my weekly food budget to the supermarket with me. I do a food shop on Monday and then, at the end of the week, I have the final third to spend on a top-up shop for necessities we may have run out of like bread and milk. I also buy the meat for the Sunday roast.

- **Do not take your bank card:** I cannot stress this highly enough. If you take your card with you it will be all too easy to use it. We have to get out of the habit of relying on cards and the easiest way to do this is to leave home without them. You have your cash budget with you and that is all you need. We have to stop thinking about what we want and focus on what we need. Take a calculator with you so you can tot up your spend as you are going around. Remember, if you use the Scan and Go option as you shop, you will have to pay by card.

- **Replenish day:** Every Monday I replenish the binder with the new week's budget. This is the moment when any money left over in the food envelope gets put into a savings challenge (see Money Challenges on page 98). This is a brilliant way to build a separate pot of cash and is so rewarding as the amount grows. It could be put towards your holiday fund or Christmas.

- **Don't get cocky:** This is not a race, it is a journey. You may feel like you have nailed your budget within a month, but it is easy to slip back into old ways. Start each week with the same respect and commitment to the process.

- **Eating in line with the budget:** After all your hard work and effort writing a list and shopping within your budget, you need to make sure the food doesn't disappear within a couple of days. This is particularly tricky if your children are stealth ninjas, like mine, and you find the occasional unauthorized snack disappearing from the cupboard.

- **Getting the kids on board:** I want to teach my children the value of money and respect for our family budget, so they are not allowed to help themselves freely in the kitchen. Instead we have dividers in the fridge so the children know what is for packed lunch and what is for grazing. I take a snack with me to school pick-up, so they don't end up in the sweet shop. In the school holidays, I put together a daily Grab Basket of snacks for each of them. This stops any arguing and once it's gone, it's gone. It also avoids us over-spending on treats when we are out.

Weekly Food Shop

I am often asked to share my weekly shopping haul on my TikTok account and I receive lots of questions about how I manage to stay on budget AND make sure nobody goes hungry. A food budget is one of my biggest successes since taking control of my money. If I stick to a routine of menu planning, strict ingredient shopping and pre-organized meals, I can stay within my budget and even have money left over at the end of each week. Here is a typical week's shop showing seven dinners and lunchbox items based on a budget of £90, bearing in mind there are a few items like breakfast cereal which I already have in the cupboard. The supermarket can remain anonymous and prices are constantly subject to change.

Monday	Toad in the Hole
Tuesday	Spaghetti Bolognese
Wednesday	Meatballs and Pasta
Thursday	Chicken Fajitas
Friday	Crispy Duck with home cooked chips
Saturday	Chilli loaded Fries
Sunday	Roast dinner

Meat
Meatballs £2.39
Lean mince 500g £2.89 (for bolognese and chilli fries)
Pack British pork sausages £1.49
Crispy duck with pancakes £6.49

Fruit & Veg
Baby button mushrooms £0.89 (for bolognese and meatballs)
Parsnips £0.62 (for the roast)
Carrots £0.49 (for toad in the hole and the roast)
Potatoes 2.5kg £1.09 (for chips with the crispy duck, mash for toad in the hole and fries with the chilli)
Cucumber £0.69 (crispy duck, lunchboxes, snack for the tortoise!)

Cauliflower/broccoli £1.19 (for toad in the hole and the roast)
Red onions £0.72 (for bolognese, chilli fries, meatballs and fajitas)
Curly kale £0.79 (for the tortoise)
Mixed chillies £0.49 (for meatballs, bolognese, chilli fries, fajitas)
Red grapes £1.75 (lunchboxes, snacks)
Bananas £0.71 (lunchboxes, snacks)

Dairy & Eggs
A dozen eggs £1.49 (for toad in the hole and Yorkshire pudding for the roast)
Semi-skimmed milk, 6 pints £2.15
Olive spread £1.09
Herb cheese spread £0.85 (sandwich filling for lunchboxes)
Mature Cheddar £2.65 (to grate over fajitas, bolognese, meatballs and chilli fries)
Yoghurts £1.19 (lunchboxes)
Cherry yoghurts £1.47 (snack)

Bread & Pasta
Medium loaf £0.39
Garlic baguette £0.32 (for meatballs)
Plain bagels £0.79 (lunchboxes)
Plain tortilla wraps £0.55 (lunchboxes)
Cheese-topped rolls x 3 £0.87 (lunchboxes)
Fusilli pasta £1.25
Spaghetti pasta £0.75

Store Cupboard

Fajita dinner kit £1.69 (use a chicken breast from the freezer)

Worcestershire sauce £0.69

Diet orange cans £1.49

Tropical juice £1.39

Spanish tomato sauce £0.99

Onion/garlic pasta sauce 0.69

Stuffing mix £0.39

Dog biscuits £1.64 (tinned meat when needed)

Toilet tissue £2.29

KitKats £1.09

Grand total = £50.85

I put the remaining £39.15 in my binder for meat for Sunday's roast and food shopping top-up towards the end of the week. This covers another pint of milk, more bread and anything that needs replenishing in the store cupboard.

Direct Debits

- **Direct debits are unavoidable:** You know this, I know this. I often get asked by people how I pay for everything by cash and the answer is, I don't. I have never said I did. I just pay for as much as I can using cash and avoid online transactions for those things I am able to. We all have to pay our mortgage, rent, council tax and energy bills via our bank account. So too our TV licence, broadband and mobile phone bills. These are set in stone (although it is always worth checking with your provider/landlord etc just to be sure) and non-negotiable. There are other costs that may be on your direct debit list, like tax bills, childcare and pension payments. Anyway, my point isn't to pay for every single thing with notes and coins, but where you can, do.

- **Interrogate your finances**: Check everything you are paying for is still valid and appropriate, like insurance, broadband or a satellite TV network. As you look at each bill find out if there is a possibility of paying for it with cash. I discovered I could do this with my water bill, for example.

- **Tax**: The US statesman Benjamin Franklin was quoted as saying, 'In this world nothing can be said to be certain, except death and taxes.' Ain't that the truth! You may be PAYE, in which case, hop along to my next point. If not, and you are self-employed, tax will hang heavily over you every year. Not only will you be paying a lump sum but you may also be paying on account ahead of money you are yet to earn. If you weren't already aware, you can set up an online account with HMRC which means you can pay in on a monthly basis and keep an eye on your debts.

- **Energy bills**: This is a large can of angry worms. There are others who are much better placed to advise on this and the ever-changing situation we find ourselves in. For my family, a Smart Meter with a dual screen displaying gas and electric usage works well and I set aside an amount each month to cover both. I pay very close attention to the meter and it gives me an exact gas cost which I can top up online. The electricity bill is an estimate and I pay it every month. I would recommend giving a monthly meter reading and paying for the electricity you use rather than being caught in the spiralling costs of direct debits.

- **Water bill benefits:** This is equally as important as the electric and gas in our home, but I was surprised it was such a hot topic on one of my TikTok videos, because of the fact I was paying this with cash. Many people opt for the direct debit plan, but I don't. The bill comes in twice a year and is based on our meter reading. While you can pay over the phone, I go straight to the Post Office with cash. I used to pay for it online, but since introducing my binder budget I now put away £35 a month ready for the bill to arrive. The amount I save is exactly what I need to cover the debt, but if I wanted to pay for it by direct debit, it would be almost twice that! If you have a water meter, ask for it to be read and get a clearer idea of usage so you can budget accordingly.

- **Pensions:** If you think this section does not apply to you because you are too young to worry about planning for old age, then think again. Skip this at your peril! If you are over twenty-two years of age and earn a minimum of £10,000 a year, then your employer is legally required to set you up on their pension scheme. You can either choose to contribute too or invest in your own private pension as a way to supplement the state amount you will receive when you retire. As with other long-term financial commitments, you need to do your homework before you decide on the best scheme or course of action. I know this feels like yet another thing you are paying out for, but a pension is the biggest saving plan of all and the one that gets most overlooked. Setting aside some additional funds each month into a pension to cushion your retirement is a positive plan of action. One of my dreams for my later years is to spend time relaxing on the sun deck of a cruise ship on an over sixties holiday. That won't happen if I don't get organized now.

- **Private health care**: I am not suggesting you need this, I am just mentioning it here as another financial commitment for long-term protection. Some are lucky enough to have this as part of their employment package, others have made a decision to invest in a private scheme. Only you know whether this is right for you and if your monthly budget can allow for it. I think it is all about priorities and this could be one of yours.

House Maintenance

Whether you own or rent your home, there are unavoidable direct debits like house insurance. Then there are the costs that jump out at you when you least expect them. Like the boiler breaking down on a cold winter morning, the washing machine packing up just as you stuff it with the school uniforms or a suspicious leak in the roof. Any one of these situations can strike fear into the heart of even the most savvy budgeter. It is hard to cover all eventualities because who knows what could happen and how much it will cost, but it's good to keep a list of possible catastrophes: boiler, white goods, structural (roof, windows, gutters), plumbing, electrics and heating, for example. Once you have assessed all the things that could break or that need maintaining, also check you have paperwork and warranties in place for those that require it. Remember, a warranty is only valid once you have activated it and does not automatically kick in with a purchase. A savings envelope with a nominal amount in each month, which – fingers firmly crossed – you may not need to call upon for some time, will ease the pain when your cooker has decided to bake its final cake.

Car Maintenance

- **Marry a mechanic:** OK, this is a joke, but Nick is actually a mechanic so, full disclosure, I don't have car maintenance bills to worry about. That said, I know exactly how to keep those costs down because he tells me.

- **Care about your car:** It's amazing how many of us use our cars as moving storage spaces or rubbish tips. Are you the sort of car owner who can find a fossilized banana skin in the pocket of the side door? A bag of melted sweets glued to the inside of the glove compartment? A pile of damp dog towels in the car boot? Or is that just my friend Lucy?! A lack of care for the interior of your vehicle could spill over to the exterior and the mechanics, so keep on top of basic maintenance. Give it a regular clean (inside and out), check the tyre pressure and pump them up if needed, check the oil and top up when necessary, and make sure you have windscreen cleaner.

- **Service history:** Make sure you get your car serviced regularly and keep the full service history up to date. This helps ensure your car continues to be roadworthy and makes a difference if you decide to sell it. Think of it as a health check for your car and a way for you to feel safer when you drive it.

- **Motor management:** Keep all your paperwork together and make a note in your calendar of when you need to pay your insurance, tax and book in for your MOT.

- **Check-up:** Before you book your car in for an MOT, get it checked over so there are no big surprises. It means you can do some work on the vehicle before the test if you are concerned it won't pass, which will help keep the cost down.

- **How to save:** In my binder, I have a folder for petrol and car insurance. I would recommend saving a monthly amount for maintenance, MOT and tax too.

- **Insurance deals:** I have always shopped around for a cheaper deal on my car insurance, but then negated the saving by paying for it on a monthly direct debit. I am not sure what took me so long to work this out! When I realized how much less I would spend if I could pay for it annually, I immediately set up a savings envelope and worked out what I needed to put away monthly to pay the full cost (based on that year's insurance). A month before my renewal date I was given a quote for over £100 more than I had paid the year before. I had no claims, so there was no reason for it to have jumped significantly. I did some digging and was amazed at the cheaper alternatives I found so I went back to my current provider to see if they could match it. In fact, the quote had been for a direct debit not the full amount and this rejig brought it back to the original figure. I know it is a big amount to pay in one go, but the money you ultimately save is so worth it.

- **Do you need to use the car every day?** Ask yourself, do I need the car for this journey? I have these things called legs, so sometimes I'll walk instead, which is better for the environment anyway . . .

Pets

To paraphrase the famous quote, pets are for life, not just for Christmas. Whether you have a dog, cat, rabbit, budgerigar, tortoise or all five, having animals is an emotional and financial responsibility. Some costs will be paid for online, like insurance, but do look at where you could set cash aside instead. This may be for food, worming tablets, flea treatments, vet bills, annual injections and kennel/cattery bills. Whatever pets you have, it is worth writing a list of their needs and factoring this as a priority into your budget.

Socializing

Are you a social butterfly who enjoys going out for dinner or catching up with friends over a bottle (or two) of your favourite red? The 'new budget you' can still do this. Having a section in your binder for this gives you an amount of cash dedicated to the joy of hitting the town. It's good to have an idea of how much you will be spending so take a look at the venue online to check their menu and drinks pricings and whether they take cash. Also find those places which offer Happy Hour and Early Bird meals – it may mean you are out on the town earlier than planned but I am a big fan of being in bed by 10pm anyway! I also love date nights, although they don't happen much since having children, but when we do go out it's great to know we aren't leaving ourselves short for important bills. I also really, really love staying in, but still want to treat myself. A takeaway curry is just as delicious eaten on the sofa, in your favourite pyjamas and fluffy slippers, as in a restaurant. The point is, you can continue to enjoy life and spoil yourself occasionally with this budget plan. It is not about deprivation, it's about moderation.

School Costs

You can swiftly skip over this section if it doesn't apply to you, but for those parents who have children in the school system or are about to, listen up. Does it sometimes feel like the school emails pinging into your inbox automatically triggers your purse to open? I can list some for you: canteen lunch (including the Christmas special), educational trips, school photos, discos, pantomime visits, coursework books and non-uniform and fundraising days. Then there is the PTA cake stall right next to the gate in the playground which is impossible to navigate a child past without buying several luridly decorated cupcakes. Don't forget the teacher contributions at the end of term or the collection for Mrs Smith, the saintly dinner lady who has been at the school since the Spam fritter days. And that's just the academic year. I haven't mentioned the growth spurts, eternal uniform updating, new school shoes (because the last pair are so tight your child's feet resemble a velociraptor's) or the trainers which replace the perfectly good pair that are now accidentally sat in another child's PE bag. I think school costs could be my specialist subject on *Mastermind*.

Once your child gets to senior school, it is harder to buy cheap and practical multipack tops in the supermarket because the entire uniform is often branded and compulsory. It is tricky to find budget-saving ways around this and now is not the time to make the kids wear one of Nan's home-knitted jumpers. Not only does the uniform change but the trips go up a level too. As well as the coach trip to Wookey Hole there are the foreign city breaks or a skiing holiday. Wouldn't we all like to take advantage of that?! Your bank account is going to take a whopping hit so best to start saving now to avoid scrimping in other areas of your outgoings later on.

Just-in-Case Fund

This is like a back-up folder of savings. A small pot of money for whatever floats your boat. It's a very personal budget envelope that you should be able to spend in a guilt-free way, whether it is for something small and regular or a big thing after many months of saving. You may want a haircut, to get your nails done, book a day at the spa, play a round of golf or buy tickets for a football match. I often use mine for home décor. Each to their own.

Gym Membership

Here is a salutary tale. Every January I would stride to the gym, convincing myself that this would be the year I would get fit. For a few weeks, I was full steam ahead and then my resolve would weaken. It was too rainy or cold. I was too tired or busy. Surely, I didn't have to go three times a week? The visits got fewer and fewer until they stopped completely, but I continued to pay my membership. I didn't cancel my direct debit because I told myself I would be going the following week. Or the one after that. We all know where this story is going. When I eventually cancelled my direct debit, I couldn't bring myself to look at how many times I had been to the gym and how much that had actually cost me. It was such a waste and a big lesson.

If the gym is your thing then great, it is worth investing in. However, if you are trying to cut back on costs then there are cheaper alternatives available. Most local colleges offer gym membership at competitive rates. Dare I even suggest a running app and a jog around the park? To be fair, nobody should be taking exercise advice from me. All I am asking is for you to be honest with yourself about the memberships you may be paying for and whether you use or need them.

Mobile Phone Contracts

I think most of us have one of these. They have become a significant part of our everyday life, whether they are a lifeline or a business tool. Love them or hate them, we all seem to need them. So how can we be smarter about how we pay for them? Most contracts run for twenty-four months, luring you with the latest device on the market. Thankfully, technology in this area isn't my strength and I just want something practical rather than fashionable. When my contract came up for renewal I didn't want to ditch my old phone so, to reduce costs, I went for a SIM-only contract. This cut my direct debit in half.

Most suppliers will have bundles and incentives to get you to sign with them. This may include TV packages for free. Do not be tempted unless they are offering things you really need. For me, the most important thing was to have good service strength in my area and high data usage so I could share it with my children on long drives. Think about what you need from your contract, not what they can offer you. You could end up paying for things that don't make a difference to your everyday life.

If your phone starts to lag and you think it needs to be upgraded, check first if it is the SIM card that is the problem. This is one of the things they don't change when you get a new phone and just pop your old SIM into its fancy new home.

Christmas

It's the most wonderful time of the year! Or so the song goes, but it can also plunge you into a spiralling financial frenzy. Particularly if you are like me and LOVE Christmas. I have always thrown festive caution to the sparkling wind throughout December and have a lovely but terrible habit of spontaneous gift giving. You can imagine the havoc that plays with the bank balance. Buying gifts makes me truly happy and to see my family's faces when they get something they really want is priceless. Except it does come with a cost attached.

It's my eldest daughter Lacey's birthday in mid-October so once we have celebrated that it is full steam ahead to Christmas. In the past, Nick and I set aside a weekend to do all the present shopping and focus on ticking things off the list, rather than keeping to a budget. It makes me feel queasy now to think that we did not plan or keep track of the full cost. When I started my financial journey, Christmas was the first major savings goal I wanted to tackle. I no longer wanted to see our bank accounts decimated so hard and fast again. I added a monthly amount to my binder and made the decision to bank it halfway through the year with a note to remind me of what was for Christmas in my account. I then carried on for the second part of the year. I now set aside the surplus money remaining from my weekly shop for Christmas (more on this tracker challenge on page 104) and once I reach my goal then I aim to save for something else.

The festive date is the same every year and yet we still panic as we approach November and the realization there may only be one or two pay days before Christmas. Not only do I save all year, I stick to a present list, buy everything by November and have it wrapped by 1st December. Sorry if I sound smug but you really should try it. It means you can enjoy every wonderful moment of the season until it is time to take the tree down. Or dismantle it. Yes, my tree is artificial but my love for the season is true.

Below are my Christmas tips for a budget-happy celebration:

- **Keep a list:** I have two lists – one for food and one for presents. I cross things off as I buy so I can keep track and make sure I am not duplicating purchases, which is all too easy to do when you panic.

- **Get organized:** Have a clear idea of what you want to buy and the cost so you can make sure your budget is in line with this.

- **Food and drink:** I start buying store cupboard items once we are in autumn and I put them away in a separate cupboard so I am not tempted to open them. Buying jars of pickle, packets of savoury snacks, tins of chocolate and wine can be done in advance and takes the pressure off a big shop the week before Christmas. Use a little of your specified budget so it doesn't come out of your weekly food shop amount. Again, this is much easier to do if you are working in cash. As you get closer to the big day you can begin to stock up on fresh ingredients, with a final shop a few days before.

- **Gifts for family and friends:** I do a similar thing for the presents and stocking treats, shopping early for great bargains and squirreling things away in a big storage box.

- **Stocking fillers:** I find this such an enjoyable thing to do, it's like having a hobby! My rule is to fill stockings with practical items like underwear, toiletries, toothbrushes, skincare and useful accessories, as well as chocolate coins and sweeties. I also create stockings for our grandchildren who are still tiny, so I include bath products and toys, a cuddle blanket, socks, accessories and books.

- **I want, doesn't always get**: I am lucky that the children don't ask for big presents and I encourage them to think hard about what they want. The remit is an item of clothing, a toy to play with, anything they enjoy, a book and something that would last. This prevents the toy catalogue being circled on every page.

- **Hamper-tastic**: For Nick's Nan and the couples in our family, I put together hampers. Another happy pastime of mine! I enjoy going to the supermarket and putting together a personalized selection of treats. You will be surprised what goodies you can buy from a pound shop to bulk it up.

- **Deck the halls**: Every year it is so tempting to buy more Christmas decorations, something I know I am guilty of. I can be easily seduced by a sparkly bauble or glittery decoration which calls to me as I walk past in search of tin foil. Not only is this expensive, it is also environmentally unsustainable to continue stocking up on bits of pretty plastic. Instead, consider treating yourself to just one or two new decorations each year and account for this in your budget.

- **Christmas deserves its own binder**: If you love Christmas as much as I do then maybe you should think about a binder dedicated to the festive season?!

Holidays

Like many families, we eagerly count down to our trip away each year, whether it is local or abroad. It's a precious opportunity for everyone to spend time together and a chance to pause in a busy year. Yes, a holiday is a luxury but one that can be achieved if you budget and save for it – which is how we approach one of our favourite US destinations, the magic that is Orlando, Florida. We go every other year if we can and tie it in with seeing family who live there, but the cost of it dictates when we can go, so we spend weeks checking various sites and dates to get the best deals. Here are a few things to consider when you are planning your holiday, wherever it may be:

- **When to book:** I'm no travel agent, but I have noticed there seems to be better times to book a holiday abroad than others. It's all down to the psychology of the shopper apparently, with companies dropping their prices midweek to entice those who may have been looking over the weekend but have not yet booked. The folk at online travel company, momondo.co.uk, go further and suggest booking a holiday on a Tuesday saves you 11 per cent. They could also be cheaper if you book in the evening rather than the morning and there are often great offers if you book a couple of months in advance. Of course, this depends on where you are going, the time of year and who you are booking with, but it is well worth paying heed to this info.

- **Ask a forum friend:** I am on social media groups for like-minded folk who also love Florida vacations and sharing great deals is a continuous hot topic. We all want value for money, even on our holibobs!

- **Binder budget:** Budgeting is in the forefront of my mind for any trip but especially for a big one like Disneyworld. I introduced a third binder specifically for the holiday and set a goal for each section I wanted to save for. It helped to take a mental walk-through of where and when my purse would come out.

- **Airport expenses:** If you are travelling in the UK then put aside an amount for service stations, train stations and stop-offs. If you are flying abroad, incorporate food, drink and duty-free into your budget. Although I save cash for the months leading up to the holiday, some airport shops only take cards, so I do bank my budget before we leave.

- **Holiday snacks:** I have a budget for incidentals on holiday, whether it is for bottles of water and crisps or breakfast on the run. It is a bit like having petty cash.

- **Food and drink:** Unless you are all-inclusive you will need to save for self-catering and/or meals out. It is worth doing your homework on where you are going, exchange rates and average food costs. City breaks always push the budget so it's good to have an understanding of cheap eats and money-saving options. Staying in an Airbnb or private rental means you can cook for yourselves rather than be beholden to the hotel or local restaurants.

- **Spending money:** In the binder, I label two folders for the children and save a small amount to hand to them at the beginning of the holiday. It not only gives them some independence, it also teaches them not to want everything on the first day. Inflatables are top of the list but if they are paying then they will be much more focused on the value of these things. As for grown-ups, we can get just as carried away with the excitement of the sun and new surroundings. Wherever we are, we are on holiday and we feel like we can indulge and deserve the treats we are eyeing up. Having a budget keeps us in line too, especially when faced with an American outlet store. Be still my beating heart!

- **Holiday wardrobe:** This can be budgeted two ways, either within the monthly budget or I save up loose coins and cash them in closer to the time. There is always a new swimsuit or sandals needed for the children as they grow so quickly.

- **Travel insurance:** Comparison markets are good at getting quotes for this. Some holiday providers offer it as an add-on to your holiday package. Don't forget to check with your bank as, depending on the account type, you may already have this included.

- **Extra costs:** It is easy to be caught out by the addition of something you didn't expect. Hotel transfers, for example. A rogue rail journey. Tickets to a show or event that you absolutely cannot miss. It is good to have a contingency envelope too, to mop these up.

Wedding Bells

Planning a wedding, or any big event, can be more stressful than you ever imagined. The big day is incredibly personal but we all want the same result: the happiest time that we and our guests will remember forever, without the debt lasting almost as long! When Nick and I got married it was around the same time as many others we knew. All of us had totally different wedding days and clearly different budgets, but we all made our celebrations unique and special to us. Ours was definitely one of the cheapest events but it was smashing. I didn't have parents who could foot the bill so it was down to Nick and I to pay for everything, with a bit of help from Nick's mum and dad. While my subconscious budget brain was severely tested, I surprised myself by how well I managed my money for the event. It was our day and our way.

We had a church ceremony and held the reception in the hall in the village where Little Nanny lived. It was a handmade wedding with a few luxuries where we wanted them. We didn't have to pay for added extras or corkage charges, for example, and I made the invitations and my sister-in-law and I made my head piece by painstakingly threading crystal beads into flower petals. We had a hundred people to the main event and a further hundred and fifty came in the evening with a fish and chip van to serve us seaside favourites and Mr Whippy ice cream for pudding. The ice cream man was called Mario and he used to sell ice cream to Nick outside his school when he was a child, so it was a nostalgic moment.

As a nod to another favourite childhood memory, my stepdad made table stands and we set up a pick-and-mix in homage to Woolworths. And our cake was in fact a hundred cakes – cup-cakes – decorated by Nick's mum. As much as I love recounting my memories of one of the best days of my life, I am sharing it here because I want you to see how it is possible to keep costs down even when entertaining a big group of people.

I think it is impossible to embark on a big event without a budget, as well as regular checks to keep on track and manage stress. Knowing your costs and being able to put money away to account for each of these is going to help you, no matter what. Some of the things to think about include venue, ceremony costs, catering, bar, entertainment, wedding favours, stationery, flowers, attire, party, transport, gifts and honeymoon. If you are about to start planning your wedding then I implore you to use the cash stuffing method as a way of saving for it. The binder really helps you stay focused for the long-term savings goal.

University

I have talked about the importance of educating children on money management and encouraging positive, healthy behaviour towards their finances. And it is for exactly this time in their lives, when they will need to utilize their knowledge. Going to university is likely to be their first true experience of managing their money and if they aren't prepared it can be a big shock to the system. Not only are they taking on a huge debt by signing up to the course, they suddenly have the responsibility of rent, bills and food to factor in each week. It is stressful enough to be away from home for the first time and thrown into a very different education system, without panicking about money too.

There is financial support but it isn't a set amount and it is means-tested. A maintenance loan can be applied for and depending on the parental financial situation and the location of the university, this determines what band you fall into and how much you are entitled to. As a parent to a child embarking on this great adventure, it is a crucial time to sit down and have a realistic conversation with them about the financial responsibilities that lie ahead. A part-time job which will earn them some money they can use as a buffer wouldn't go amiss right now. Ideally, they would have started this while they were in sixth form so could have been saving for a while. It is always better to be prepared than to be surprised.

Some students may not receive as much financial support as they realistically need and although family circumstances are factored in, this does not mean they are able to pick up the financial shortfall. Setting a budget plan with your child is the perfect way to not only share guidance but to also give them a good indication of what is ahead. Don't expect the maintenance loan to land in the bank account on the first day of Freshers' Week either. I have seen people freaking out because they are chasing their child's finance and students trying to track down their money, with no safety net to fall back on. As you know by now, I love a list, so here are a few helpful points for consideration:

- Freshers' Week is when the students settle in, get to know their surroundings and meet potential roomies or flat families. Every university plans theirs in different ways. There is often the purchase of a wrist band to cover all the events planned for that week including day trips, themed parties, catering and bar. It is a rite of passage but it comes at a financial cost. Saving in advance for this helps.

- Rent is a fundamental cost and it is important to find out whether utilities are included and how this will be split between flatmates.

- Food shopping is a minefield. Not only do they need to eat healthily but they may have limited culinary skills. At some universities, you can pay extra to be in catered accommodation. I hear the typical diet is beans on toast, pasta and noodles!

- Let's not pretend our hard-working students are all graft and no play. There may be a subsidized bar for cash purchases and pre-booked events are likely to be paid for online so they will need money in the bank too.

- There may be transport to and from the campus but there will definitely be trips home to factor in and this can either be relatively affordable coaches or more expensive train journeys. As long as there is enough space for them to return with mounds of washing!

- Personal care and clothing are also on the list. I would like to encourage all students to visit their local charity shops regularly, because you can get the best bargains and pick up some great vintage pieces too. It is also the first place to source a themed outfit for a fancy dress party.

- Not all textbooks and course material are provided on certain courses. This is something to bear in mind and budget for.

5

Money Challenges

Setting yourself a saving challenge is a fantastic way to scoop up any unspent cash from your previous month's budget and add it to a special pot. There are times when I am lucky if I have more than a handful of shrapnel left over, but rather than leaving it in my purse, I want it to be useful. Depending on your income and what you budget to save in your binder, you may have a few coins that can be added to a challenge or goal. When I began this crazy saver's journey, I was fascinated by how many other people tackled their budgets in a variety of ways, often incorporating additional challenges to keep them on track. It is a successful approach if you want to save for something particular. I knew I would do the same once I had settled into the cash stuffing process and was keen to find a challenge which didn't dictate the amount I would need to invest.

Although I waited until I felt budget-confident, taking on a challenge can be a good way to ease yourself, or others, in to the idea of saving. If the thought of cash stuffing feels overwhelming then you could start with one of these fun money-saving experiments instead. They are also an excellent way to introduce children to a savings plan and get them motivated. It is a fun, rewarding experience and a brilliant opportunity to teach them more about money management.

You can find trackers and challenge sheets online or you can make your own one (I've also included one at the back of this book). I have since taken on a few challenges and I LOVE THEM. I think you will too.

The Flexible-Envelope Savings Challenge

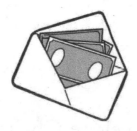

This is my absolute favourite! There is no set amount, hence the wonderful 'flexible' in the title. I simply put any remaining money left over from my previous week's food budget into an envelope. You don't have to have a plan of what you are saving for or a deadline for stopping. It's not money you would be 'missing' because you had already budgeted to spend it, so rather than waste it, put it away.

A few weeks into my first challenge I decided I was going to buy a watch for Nick, which kept me motivated and excited to see how much I could save. It also encouraged me each week as I was eager to replenish my food folder so I could take the remaining money from the week before and stuff my savings envelope. I keep a note to see how much money is going in.

The 52-Week Envelope Challenge

You will need 52 envelopes. Write a set amount on each. The figure is entirely up to you. You then jumble up the envelopes and pull one out each week. Whichever one you pull out that week has to be stuffed with the exact amount. They can be as small or as big as you think you can realistically manage. You can take the jeopardy out of the process and simply write £10 on each, which will give you £520 at the end of your challenge.

The 1–100 Envelope Challenge

This challenge has the same principles as the above, except the numbers do not duplicate. You will need 100 envelopes. On each envelope, you need to write 1, 2, 3, 4 all the way up to 100. You can keep them in numerical order or spice it up by mixing them. Each envelope needs the number of pounds as stated, whether it is

£1, £2, £3 and so on. Depending on your finances you could leave this for a couple of weeks, or pull out two in one go, as there is no deadline to worry about. The only caveat to this is whether you are prepared to pay £99 should you pull out the envelope with that number on it. Once all the envelopes are filled you will have saved an amazing £5050.00.

The Penny-Savings Challenge

This requires a bit of commitment as the challenge has to be completed every day for an entire year. On the first day you add 1p to the jar, on the second day it is 2p and you keep going until you have hit day 365 and added £3.65. If it is a leap year then you don't need to add an extra day, you just complete the task a day earlier. Incredibly, this challenge, which will have minimal impact on your purse, will help you save a very welcome £667.95

The £2 Challenge

The £2 is the coin I love the most because it is double the value of the £1 and rarer to come by, hence increasing the thrill of saving them! Of course, this challenge can be easily done with any coin of your choice, but if you want the most out of your savings, avoid using coins below 50p. You will need a terramundi pot – a piggy bank which has to be broken to get the money out of it. This is an ingenious, old-fashioned way to prevent you from dipping in to your savings. Every time you are in possession of a £2 coin, pop it in the pot and forget about it. Once the pot is full you can open it. I highly recommend wrapping the pot in a tea towel and placing it in a carrier bag before you smash it, to prevent ceramic shards going everywhere. I have used the terramundi technique in the past to save money for a holiday and was amazed to hit £600. Don't blame me if this begins an obsession with the shiny and satisfying coin. I will admit to swapping coins with a friend for a £2 in her purse.

Money-Saving Bingo

Create twenty-five boxes – five rows of five boxes and write any amount you feel comfortable with. For explanation purposes, let's say each box has £20 written on it. The aim of this challenge is to see how many boxes you can fill in the quickest time, giving you a nice little bingo win of £500 at the end of the process.

The NO-SPEND challenge

This is not for the faint-hearted. It requires willpower but it is great for those who gravitate towards their card and want the motivation to reset old habits. This challenge is different from the rest as you don't put any money away, you just cut down on any additional spending. You stick to the necessities and whatever you have budgeted for and nothing more. No cheeky takeaways, no coffee shops – no treats basically. Some people do this for a week and others a month, or more. Ultimately, a no-spend challenge does need a reward, something to look forward to at the end of the frugal slog. Maybe that pair of shoes you really wanted or a slap-up dinner out.

The Trackers

A tracker is a visual printout of monetary values to document your savings. They are a bit like the rewards card that you are given in coffee shops which get stamped with each purchase, or like a child's reward chart system. They can be for different amounts or a set of £5, £10 or £20 and you cross off each box as you save the designated value. If challenges are not your thing, trackers are a great way of keeping on top of additional goals. They can be tailored to your personal savings binder or used alongside a terramundi which helps you remain focused and on track. I love utilizing a tracker system with my Christmas savings goal. Ostensibly they are another sort of list that keeps note of the money as you put it away. There are so many out there, you just need to look online to discover a tracker world of different designs and personalized options. Or make your own and laminate it, so you can use a Sharpie, wipe it clean at the end of the challenge and start again.

It is a great visual tool to refer to, to see how much you have saved to date and what is remaining until you hit your target amount. I have both a £10 tracker and a £20 tracker and combined they help me reach my saving goal of £900 for Christmas. Any surplus money I have left over from my weekly food shop, as well as money remaining in my socializing and just-in-case folder, goes towards filling my tracker each month. I technically have 30 weeks to do this but I love completing things earlier so I can move onto my next potential savings goal. These trackers are not date-specific like some of the other challenges so an 'as and when' approach is the best way to utilize them.

6

How to Make Money
(with what you already have)

For many of us, the thought of budgeting and saving money feels fantastical because we just don't have it to begin with. We may be living off credit cards, agonisingly overdrawn, struggling with outgoings larger than our income or, in too many heartrending cases, choosing whether to heat the room or eat a meal. It is hard to budget in these circumstances and impossible to save money we don't have. My childhood was the perfect example of this so I completely understand how many ways we can get caught out financially. Telling someone to tighten their belt when there is nothing left to cut back on or suggesting they should just get more work must rank amongst the top most useless, unempowering and thoughtless things to say in this situation.

So, I wanted to share some ideas that could be helpful. Not the sort that suggests you trek to the end of the rainbow, in the hope you will discover a glowing pot of gold, but some practical pointers that you may not be aware of.

Interrogate Your Finances

I am awfully fond of saying this but I am forever surprised at the number of people who do not question long-term direct debits, increasing costs and the relevance of standing orders. If you haven't done this already, look at every repeat payment which leaves your account and check you are not paying for a membership, insurance or commitment which is no longer valid. Check you can cancel immediately without incurring a penalty. Also be aware of those clever little apps which lure you in on a free trial period and take your payment details. There will be no reminder from them on the day of cancellation, nor will they alert you to the payment. They will just start taking your money from you. If the money you have saved doesn't have an instant alternative use, then you could use it for a savings challenge instead.

Tax May Be Taxing

Following on from my first point, are you sure you are paying the correct council tax? And are you on the right tax code? If you are freelance, are you claiming all the appropriate expenses? Have you found out which benefits you may be eligible for? A lot of questions, I know, but worth finding the answers online to check your position.

Shop Around

Just because you have a bank account and various insurances it doesn't mean you must stick with what you have. Look around for the best deals on all financial matters to make sure yours still work for you. Some bank accounts offer a lump sum if you decide to switch so it is well worth considering, especially if you aren't happy with where you currently are.

Seasonal Work

If you are looking to earn extra cash, but are unable to commit to something long term, then part-time, casual or project-based work could be for you. The lead-up to Christmas is always a good time to find something in hospitality or retail. If you live in or near a tourist destination, there are often opportunities so keep an eye out or pop in to the places most likely to need additional staff. Supermarkets are a great place to start and offer fair rates of pay and food discounts.

Vouchers, Coupons and Loyalty Points

Make your chosen supermarket (or several) work for you by taking advantage of any offers they have. By this, I do not mean BOGOFs or bulk buys, I mean coupons you can use, signing up for the loyalty card or benefiting from a voucher system. Each store has a different approach so spend the time investigating what else you can gain from your weekly shopping basket.

Sell, Sell, Sell

Have a big sort out at home. Not only will you feel better once you have tidied up cupboards, but you may find you have items of value. Selling via eBay, Vinted, Depop or Facebook Marketplace are a brilliant way to earn some cash and declutter at the same time. Get the children to go through their toys and clothes too. You could even make a day of it and have a stall at a car boot sale. There are also specific sites online which will buy books, DVDs, CDs and even

Lego by the kilo. This is exactly the sort of recycling I love and a great way to avoid things ending up in landfill.

Spare Room Rental

If you own your own property or have the appropriate rental agreement and you have a spare room, you could rent it out. Some people have been known to rent their garages to those who don't have one and even their front drives for parking. Alternatively, you could rent out your whole house or flat on Airbnb or a similar website. This works exceptionally well if you live in a tourist area or town where they hold big sporting or music events that will attract fans, but don't discount it if you don't. People may be looking for somewhere to stay for work or family reasons too.

Lisa's Fridge-Magnet Money Manifesto

When embarking on a new plan or regime, I find it really helpful to write out a handy list of dos and don'ts to keep me on track. Here are my often-repeated mottoes which you could write out and stick on the fridge or the mirror if you need a reminder of what you are doing and why. I have also attached a little explanation to each one, but there's no need to add all this too, unless you want to paper the wall of the loo.

Saving Something is Better Than Nothing

You do not need loads of money to start cash stuffing. Nor do you need a set amount each week or month. When your finances are stretched, put away what you can, even if it's just a fiver. A little each time will keep the momentum and help you focus. Take it slow and let it grow.

You Can Be a Basic Budgeter

Stop believing you have to be a mathematical wizard, or Rachel Riley, to know how to budget. Instead, keep it simple and use stationery rather than technology. Build your number-crunching confidence with just a pen, paper and calculator. Working out your figures will give you all you need to devise your personal budgeting goals.

Cash Not Card

My bank card is no longer my automatic default when paying for things. While the majority of us use debit and credit cards, we shouldn't rely on them in every area of our lives. Spending real money keeps me accountable for what goes out and what is left.

Leave your card safely in your wallet or at home, so you are not tempted to use it when you don't need to.

Exploring Equals Expense

Ever popped into the supermarket for a few items and come out with two bags full?! Then this reminder is for you. It is so easy to get distracted and lost in consumer heaven. Before you know it, you have overspent on things you didn't really need. Stop making life hard for yourself and stick to the shopping list you have carefully planned.

Actions Not Excuses

'I'm not good with money!' is something I hear all the time and it is the worst reason for not changing your money mindset. Consider why you think that and tell the negative voice to pipe down. Have you ever given yourself the chance to try and be better? There is no exam to take when it comes to handling your finances, you just need to understand your incoming money, your outgoing spending habits and what you can save. Only you can change your approach to money and find a more stress-free way of living. Grow that confidence whilst growing your savings at the same time.

If I Can, You Can

I had no guidance growing up. I spent years in complete denial about my financial affairs. I assumed this was just what life was and accepted my fate. It wasn't until my early forties that a random TikTok post ignited the realisation that I could change my attitude to money and benefit from it. I am just me – a mum and a wife – and in a relatively short amount of time I took control of something that had been controlling me my entire life. It's not about having a talent or gift for money and luck certainly plays no part. What I have done is totally achievable for most of us.

Once You Top Up, You Just Can't Stop

At the risk of repeating myself, I LOVE my binders and how much they have supported my money-saving way of life. I can visually see my finances grow every time I top up the envelopes. The amount will only go down if I remove the money and that is not going to happen unless it is spent for its original purpose. Topping up these folders is satisfying and rewarding, and becomes addictive, which keeps me focused on my end goal. As habits go, this is a good one to have.

Don't Be Run by Robots

Who remembers the cartoon *The Jetsons*, about a family living a futuristic sci-fi life? It was funny and faintly ridiculous but sometimes I feel like we are in one of the episodes. As appealing as a more computerized future is for various reasons, like convenience, these are also the things that will backfire. I wish we could all slow down and reflect on how often technology makes decisions for us. We need to make sure we are in control and get the best out of the new world, rather than the other way around.

Stick to the List

You know how important lists are in my life – without them I would have struggled to make my budget work. It's perfectly easy to work out a plan and write it down, but what can be hard is sticking to it. This may sound obvious, but I am going to say it: once you have written a list, remember to look at it. I am speaking from early experience. Whether it is for your overall budget plan, the weekly food shop or the Christmas presents, going off-piste and disregarding the list is likely to cost you money. Stay on track.

Stop Riding the Rollercoaster of Credit and Debit

Our emotions are affected by our financial stability. We all enjoy the highs associated with having money and despair of the lows when the coffers are empty. To make ourselves feel better we may go into debt, use credit cards or borrow money to get us out of the hole we are in. After all, it is only temporary, isn't it? And then we are on a stomach-lurching rollercoaster of our own making. Putting a budget in place means we can get onto a secure and steady footing with our accounts, and jump the finance rollercoaster for good.

Budgets Don't Have to be Boring

Budgets get a bad reputation and are thought of as negative, mean and constricting. In fact, they are a helpful, practical and positive way of looking after our money. Somewhere, somehow the narrative changed and the meaning behind the word got lost in translation. Bring back the budget in all its beneficial glory!

Use it Or Lose It

Can you imagine what life would be like without actual, physical money?! This could be what happens if we continue to rely on making virtual and digital purchases. Tapping away may be easy, but it won't help when you want to assist the Tooth Fairy or contribute your change to the charity pot on the shop counter. I know recent, unprecedented times have sped up our reliance on other forms of payment, but we need to keep using cash when we can. Let's not be responsible for a cashless society and all the issues that come with that.

Moderation not Deprivation

We imagine that sticking to a budget means restricting the things we enjoy – and yet it means the complete opposite. When we have a handle on our finances we can still treat ourselves now and again. Admittedly, it won't be all the time and we will need to save up instead of purchasing instantly, but that is what got us in trouble in the first place. Paying for things as you buy them rather than paying off something you had long forgotten about is enjoyment in itself. Decide what you want, set a goal, save up and then spend it, safe in the knowledge that it isn't going to bankrupt you in the process. Budgets don't mean no, they mean wait until you have the funds.

Stash the Cash

For me, holding money helps me save it. Once I have it and I can see it, I don't want to waste it. A bit like a squirrel hoarding its haul of nuts ready for a long winter, I stash my cash in my binder. Living from month to month and ignoring my bank statements didn't work for me. Physically touching, counting and sorting my cash really does. Seeing is truly believing.

7
Lisa's Life Hacks

Look, I am certainly no life guru, nor do I claim I invented these hacks, but I wanted to share some handy hints for making sure your money lasts longer. This is all about keeping your money in your binder and not wasting it unnecessarily. You may already do some of these things, but if not, it is worth trying them out. No need to thank me. I've got your back.

Snack Time at Home

Do your little ones spend most of the school holidays asking for food? Honestly, how do my children function on a school day, because last time I looked classrooms were not equipped with fully stocked snack cupboards! Yet my two youngest children behave like they have to eat all day. To prevent guarding the kitchen during their waking hours, I introduced a snack basket. I place a few different items, be it a packet of crisps, some fruit, a chocolate bar and a snack bag, in the basket. Each child has their own. This is not a meal replacement but a grab-and-go for those peckish in-between moments. Trying to make food last is no longer a losing battle.

Sweetie Hack for the Walk Back

No sooner have you met your little angels in the playground and they instantly need feeding. It's not 'Nice to see you, Mum,' it's 'What's for snack?' swiftly followed by 'What's for tea?' It doesn't help if the local ice cream man is parked outside your school. This becomes a costly affair and one I needed to tackle quickly as part of my food-shop-budget plan. Fear not, I have the answer. Throw those welcoming arms wide as your children run towards you, safe in the knowledge that you have snacks in your pocket, brought from home. KitKats, Freddos or apples can be bought in multipacks and divvied up throughout the week. With any luck, they will be too busy chewing to notice the queue for Mr Whippy.

Halve your Meat and Double your Dish

We can easily fall into the trap of cooking too much food, putting the leftovers in the fridge and then finding them again a week later. I have been guilty of over-catering in the past and making too much for one mealtime, but not enough for two nights. I was also over-reliant on meat in many of the dinners I cooked, which has cost and environmental implications. It is so much better for us to eat less meat for various reasons. Now I use less meat and bulk up a dish with plenty of vegetables, such as peppers, onions and root veg. I cut meatballs in half and freeze what's left for a dish the following week. I do the same with mincemeat and chicken. You could even batch cook and freeze so there is a ready-made meal for the following week. There is very little waste now and my food bill is lower too.

Bathroom Behaviour

This may be too much information, but I am convinced my family use more toilet roll when they can see a pile of them in the bath-room, like a 'free for all' neon sign. I don't know how we ever got through so many at such an alarming rate. Short of sitting my children down and interrogating them on loo paper usage, I decided to hide the rolls instead. Now they are in the airing cupboard and they aren't disappearing so quickly. Riddle me that! It could be a complete coincidence, but give it a go. Maybe there is something in the psychology of seeing an abundance and assuming it will always be so. It also means my children use a cloth to clean up a spill rather than reams of loo paper.

The Concentrated Approach to Cleaning

I don't think I am alone in having favoured cleaning products, especially if they are disinfectants with a seasonal scent. Here's an idea that may help your pocket and save on a little bit of cupboard space too: opt for the concentrated version. Yes, it requires diluting, but it lasts four times as long as a pre-measured bottle, for the same price.

Washing Machine Time

When I got my washing machine, I made the schoolgirl error of thinking I knew exactly what I was doing. After all, I have been using a washing machine since I was a teenager. As long as I could put the detergent in and start the thing, that was all I needed to know, right? Well, no. I was wrong, very wrong. I thought a 40-degree wash was the standard practice until I hit my forties. I may have had a cold wash button, but I never used it. Now I rely on it with every general wash I do. Not only is this better for the planet, but I am saving money by no longer needing to heat water on a cycle. I have also noticed my white items stay white and they smell freshly washed. I have told everyone I know, so now I am telling you. Opt for a lower temperature and love your laundry!

Drying the Clothes

When the weather gets colder and the rain comes, we all turn to inside drying hacks, like placing a clothes airer upstairs if your home layout allows, as heat rises. I give heavier garments, such as towels and denim, an extra spin just to reduce the water content and make sure they dry quicker. If you have an airing cupboard, you could get yourself a sock peg holder, pop your undergarments on it and leave it in the cupboard. I found with a family of four, a lot of space was taken up with a million pairs of socks before I had hung anything else out. Alternatively, try placing a bed sheet over your airer and over the radiator to help direct the heat onto your clothing, or try a heated airer. There are lots of reviews online about which are the best. We do have a tumble dryer and in emergency situations it gets used if items need a quick turnaround. I only tumble for twenty minutes and then take the items out and shake them individually before popping them back in if more time is needed. You could be wasting unnecessary electricity on clothes that are in fact bone dry yet still spinning around in the drum.

Lead-Up List at Christmas

It's not just Santa who has a list. Hand on festive heart, using a Lead-Up List for Christmas has been a total game changer, for both my purse and my stress levels. We all know it should be a jolly ol' time and starting early doesn't spoil the magic or mean you are crazy; it means you are taking control. I write down all the treats our family enjoys, including non-perishables and decorative items like Christmas crackers, wrapping paper etc. I do the same with stocking items for each of my family members. Every week I try and get as much as I can ticked off using my surplus food-shopping money and within a month I have amassed a stockpile. If storage is an issue then dedicate a cupboard in the kitchen or a cardboard box to these items. I get this all bought with many weeks to spare, with only the fresh produce to do the week of Christmas itself. It also saves that massive Christmas shop and prevents panic when you can't find any pickles on the shelf. Believe.

Black Friday Feels

This is a difficult day to navigate. I love Black Friday, but I always approach it with caution and stick to what I need. There are great deals out there, but there are also many more that pretend to be saving you money. I do my homework beforehand so I know that I am getting the best price. This takes some time and effort but it is worth it, particularly if you need to replace anything electrical like your TV or vacuum cleaner. Be strict, stay on course and do not be seduced. If Black Friday is a big date in your calendar and a way to do all your Christmas shopping, then why not use an envelope in your binder to save up for it?

Gift Giving

Party gifts can come at a cost, especially if it's a school friend and your child wants to head to the toy shop to find something special.

And expensive. So, I started using the same method regardless of age and it's been a huge hit. In fact, now it is expected. It is very simple. I fill a cupcake box (which has a clear window) with sweets. Depending on the number of parties that month, it might be cheaper to grab a bigger variety pack of mixed treats and create multiple boxes at one time. I then place the birthday card inside and wrap it with ribbon to seal. You will need individually sealed sweets to prevent the contents going stale. I mean, who doesn't like to receive a mixed box of sweets? Even the adults I've gifted them to loved them. You can get the boxes in multipacks and although I budget £10 per gift, the sweet-treat boxes can be made for approximately £5 when using a four-piece cupcake box. One day I hope to get given one. Or maybe I will just make one for myself . . .

Organize your Kitchen Cupboards

I am sorry if I am using the word 'organized' too much, but trust me it really does help. Knowing what is in your kitchen cupboards could potentially save you money and prevent waste. I use clear containers to group together items that used to get lost in our Narnia-inspired cupboards. It not only saves time when I am foraging for that all-important ingredient, it also prevents overbuying on things you already have but didn't know you did. How many of us have found three tubs of the same gravy granules in different locations? No need to answer that. One swift stock take, and you'll save time and money on your shopping list. Bulk buying is out, storage containers are in. Word.

Nice nails . . .

. . . But no budget to maintain them. This is me to an absolute T. I like having beautiful nails, but I'm a nail technician's nightmare. I love them at first, the long length, polished finish, but I never commit to having the refills, and by the time I see growth and separation I want them off. A total waste of money in my opinion. I purchased the box sets that you glue on at your own leisure, but, again, after a few days they went ping, ping, ping, popping off all around the house. So, I bought a home nail lamp and gel polish and got to work doing my nails for occasions that required the glam look. It saved me money and lasts a lot longer than the previous two options. If you're not good at polish self-application then definitely check out some great hacks online that show you how to create a barrier around the nail to prevent overspill.

Don't Knock It Until You've Tried It

I was all for brands and pretty packaging, but now I am a complete convert to supermarket own-brand versions. I knew it would take the kids longer to adapt to the new products and they would be instantly put off if their favourite cereal didn't have the usual characters on their boxes, or biscuits didn't have logos they recognized. So, I put it to the test. I transferred the cereal into a breakfast decanter, exactly like the ones you see at the hotel breakfast buffet, and I hid the cardboard box in the recycling. I emptied the biscuit packets into Tupperware. I do this with sauces too. If my sister-in-law ever reads this, I have a confession to make: Emma, you know how you think the ketchup we serve alongside our barbeques is the branded version – the only one you say you like? Well, it isn't. In fact, it is the lower-priced one, decanted into a bottle. No doubt she will bring her own from now on! Be more me: buy the lower-cost alternative and say nothing. We make ourselves believe that the brand is better and we are willing to pay the price they dictate, but if you are serious about money saving, then buying cheaper alternatives is a great way to cut your food bills.

Home Is Where the Heart Is

Budgeting doesn't mean you can't have a pretty home. I love to refresh the house annually with paint re-coats or touch up any tired-looking woodwork. It won't surprise you to hear I always look around for the best deals when I am about to do a room makeover, from wallpaper in the reduced bin to last season's must-have cushions. I always set a budget to work with to ensure I don't get carried away with the project. I've saved hundreds so far with upcycling furniture. You may be surprised with how a side table looks after it is sanded down and given a fresh coat of paint. I avoided buying new kitchen tops and spent just £40 recovering mine with new vinyl instead. Always look at the 'how to' videos online and trust yourself enough to have a go at some DIY, because it is amazing what you can achieve (with the caveat that nobody should be touching their electrics). Charity shops and good old-fashioned car boot sales can uncover some absolute beauties, things that others no longer need. As a general note, I wouldn't try and haggle with the seller because they are already selling things very cheaply. Yet again, these ideas can save you money and save the mountains of unwanted stuff we churn out every year.

Plan Your Journeys

I may be a little late to the party, but since I have started budgeting for petrol, I am now much more conscious of fuel consumption. In the past I would jump into the car at the mere mention of posting a package, popping to the shops for a pint of milk or running random errands across town. When the fuel light shone on the dashboard, I would head straight to the petrol station and fill up the car. I always considered it a necessity and didn't count the number of times I was back at the pumps. Not any more! Now I plan my journeys around the shortest, most cost-effective route and group my errands accordingly. Rather than going back and forth on a whim like some sort of mundane crystal maze challenge, I save time and fuel by combining my chores and taking fewer, more practical routes. Being organized means fewer returns to do the things I had forgotten about first time around and I can see the positive impact of this in my petrol budget. I walk more too.

I know there are times this approach is not the answer – if you are travelling to and from your place of work, for example. However, if there are alternatives out there, like car shares with colleagues or bus travel, then try them. Your employer may offer a bike2work scheme if that's practical. The school run is deadly because everyone plans to walk and then runs out of time and can't face dragging their little angels along the pavement. You could incorporate a scooter into their gift list and make walking fun in nice weather. Disclaimer: I do in fact drive to school when it is raining. I hate the idea of them sitting in soggy tights and damp uniforms all day.

Birthday Parties

I love to host a birthday party for my girls, but the cost can rise the minute the date is confirmed. Suddenly, your child wants to invite the entire class, not to mention cousins and the offspring of close friends. What started as a low-key party might turn into a big-budget gala event if you allow it.

I give my children a maximum of thirty children on their invitation list and keep the cost low with budgeting hacks I have learned along the way. Of course, it is cheaper to host the party at home and this works with smaller numbers, but a local hall can be as affordable as £10 an hour. I book a hall and focus on addressing the two most important costs: food and entertainment.

I have gone overboard with food in the past and felt that not only should we be feeding the little guests but also their parents and any additional siblings who may be loitering. At the end of the party, I felt like crying as I emptied the food waste into a big rubbish bag. To avoid over-catering, I now use a simple method of party platters, strategically placed in the middle of the tables to accommodate groups of six children. They have a selection of every type of party food a child dreams of, like sandwiches, mini sausages, fruit, cupcakes and crisps. I fill jugs with fruit juice, rather than giving out individual cartons, and write the name of each child on their paper cup to prevent mix-ups and tears. I make up an extra platter for the parents to enjoy and supplement this with anything the kiddies didn't touch. Waste not want not is my party motto.

When it comes to entertainment, I keep it very simple. Make

a playlist of all the latest child-appropriate songs and link it to a speaker. If they want to have a disco they can, if not the music is useful for some of the party games you may wish to play, like musical statues, bumps or chairs! The oldies are still the goodies. Face-painting can be costly, but not if you make some requests at quote time, with a theme in mind. Prevent hiring the artist for the full length of the party by agreeing on one design beforehand. Not only does this mean they will whizz through all the children much faster, they will also be there for less time, making the booking cheaper. After one of our parties, the children left with beautiful rainbows painted on their faces – and so did some of the parents!

FAQs

Here are questions I am asked most often. I go into more detail throughout the book, but I thought it might be useful to single out those queries that come up again and again, and to have all the answers here in one place. This is also a good section to revisit once you have read the book and need to refresh your mind on any points.

Where did you get your binders from?

I bought mine from Amazon, but you can also purchase them from eBay and Etsy, to name a couple of outlets. Just look up 'cash binder' or 'money saving wallet' online. There are so many different versions in amazing colours, and, in some cases, you can even have them personalized.

How do I use cash stuffing when so many places state 'card-only payments'?

This is something I have yet to have an issue with in my everyday life, but I know of instances where others have come unstuck. I do understand the frustration when you are trying to pay with cash and are told it is not possible. I would recommend planning ahead so you know where and who will take real money. I never have a problem paying for food, retail purchases or certain bills at the post office, for example. When we have a family day out, I check ahead to make sure visitor attractions, venues etc will take cash, to avoid any disappointment.

What about direct debits?

Amounts for the direct debits remain in the bank every month until they are paid out. All the bills are paid within the first week of the month, which helps with knowing exactly how much I have left, even after deducting the food shopping each week.

What is a sinking fund?

A sinking fund is an amount of money set aside for a specific upcoming expense, such as Christmas, birthdays, car insurance, or a big event like a wedding or a holiday. It can be anything you feel would help with these one-time large amounts being paid out and enable you to spread the cost over a period of time. Think of it as anything you want to save for, which is not tied to a direct debit.

Do you divide all your surplus money up into the binders?

Each envelope in my binder has a grand total, so I know exactly what I need to contribute at the beginning of every month. The surplus money remains in my bank account to cover any additional costs that may accrue or emergency payments not taken into account beforehand. I like seeing it slowly grow in my bank too, so I try my best not to touch it.

Are you concerned about having all that money in the house?

My initial response is no, I am not. The money is in a safe and the safe is hidden. I think people assume I just keep adding to it and they forget money is also removed. When the amounts become bigger, I may deposit them into the bank, depending on what they are earmarked for. I also have short-term savings for specific goals, all of which will be spent and the envelope emptied ready for a new goal.

You must have to earn loads of money to be able to budget?

This is simply not true. The method of budgeting is to be able to have control of your income and ensure you are covering all your outgoings by using a system that works for you, in order to set aside money for future expenses. Some use budgeting to make sure they can live paycheck to paycheck, others use the method to help save up for hobbies, luxuries or be organized if they are planning a big event, like their own wedding. As I always say, focus on the method, not the money.

How do you get the cash? Are you paid in cash, or do you work cash in hand?

The money I add into my binders is withdrawn from my bank account. Weekly for some, like my food bill, and monthly for some, like my sinking funds.

How do you stop using your card? It's so hard to break the habit of grab, go and tap!

That is exactly what it is, a bad habit that we choose not to think about and one I wish I could help everyone deal with. It is a continual battle to leave the card alone, but this journey has helped me realize that the convenience of a card takes away so much control. Most of us do not register our purchases on a daily basis and this is how problems grow. Organization, leaving your card at home and a little bit of willpower help.

How much money do you take out for your binder, and do you withdraw more if you run out?

I can't overstate how important organization is to the budget process. It is crucial to know exactly what you need for the month ahead to avoid any pitfalls. 'Fail to plan, plan to fail' is a good motto to remember when it comes to money management. I always plan for the next month in advance, and I like to know about birthdays, events and school trips to ensure I am budgeting as realistically as possible. I hate last-minute surprises. I have two envelopes in my binder (socializing and just-in-case fund), which I use for myself or the children to cover any spontaneous spends we may make. So far, the amount I add to them seems sufficient and I have not had to top it up.

Would children benefit from having a binder?

Educating and encouraging children to understand money is one of my favourite discussion points. I think it's really important that the younger generation are taught budgeting skills, be it using a binder with actual cash, a money box, a pocket money chart or an online system. Having experience with notes and money is preferable, for all the same reasons as us adults. The less we all handle money, the more we are detached from the value it holds and we struggle to visualize and appreciate the cost of things. By showing a child exactly what can be bought for £5, it might make them realize it is more than just a blue piece of paper. It also teaches them goal-setting and gives them that wonderful feeling of achievement when they reach their target and buy the thing they have saved so hard for.

How did you come to £90 a week for your food budget?

When I first tackled my finances, I could see I was spending around £120 on food alone without all the other additional items that fell into my trolley. I knew I had to cut down, so I wrote out a meal plan for the week and a shopping list of ingredients I needed. I knew it would be less than my usual bill, but I wasn't sure by what exactly, so I took £90 with me. I stuck to the list and what I didn't spend was put back in the binder, ready to cover any additional top-ups, like bread, milk, butter etc, later in the week. To see £25 left over in that very first week was fantastic. It was the same the week after and the next, so I kept to that amount and it remains our weekly food allowance.

What does your weekly £90 food budget cover?

My weekly food shop covers food, packed lunch items, snacks, pet food, personal care products and cleaning products. I don't have to buy everything every week, but I keep a note of what I am running low on.

What meals do you cook each week on a £90 budget?

Firstly, each household's needs and tastes are different, and it also depends on the number of people that budget has to cover, personal dietary requirements and income. I will admit I am not the most exciting cook, but we enjoy simple meals like pasta bakes, toad in the hole, roast dinners and spaghetti bolognese. It helps if you cut down on meat, ready meals and branded items too.

Do you meal prep?

I don't prepare meals, I plan our meals. Batch cooking would be amazing if only I had the room to store frozen dinners. Our menu is not dictated to by certain days either, so we don't live from a pre-written board. I write the seven meals we will eat that week and ensure I have almost everything I need when I return from my Monday food shopping trip. I usually hold off on buying the meat for Sunday, as the sell-by dates are sometimes on the day or the day after and I prefer to cook fresh (not frozen) when it comes to a joint of meat.

Each day I cook a meal we all like, knowing I have everything to hand. Some meal ingredients can be altered slightly to create a different dish, without the need to go out and purchase more food. Take sausages, for example, which can be transformed into a toad in the hole, served with mash, added into a pasta bake or popped into a casserole. Having a look through a few cookbooks or online for ideas really helps too. TikTok sensation Mitch Lane – @mealsbymitch – is the self-styled 'King of Fiver Meals' and does a brilliant job of showing his followers how to make delicious meals on a budget.

Why don't you bulk-buy? Would it not reduce shopping trips and help with overspending?

I was a weekly bulk-buyer! That was one of the approaches that got me into trouble. I went armed with a trolley and a blank space between the ears. Every week I picked up items I already had and sometimes multiple items, especially cleaning and personal care products. I also tried to do a monthly shop while continuing to visit the supermarkets regularly. I was stockpiling for whatever the future might hold. A therapist may argue this was because the cupboards were empty when I was growing up and I subconsciously needed to see them full. I did have a fascination with American couponing too, but lacked a basement to hold all my purchases and didn't take any coupon vouchers. As I still needed fresh produce weekly, I couldn't stop myself picking up things that weren't necessary. There are occasions when bulk-buying works well, especially if you have a large family to cater for and the deals are good. Just be sure you can reap the benefits.

What about online shopping such as Amazon? Where do the funds come from for that?

My online purchases are not budgeted within my binder. I have worked hard to cap my online spending, especially with Amazon, and I now use it in a very limited way. The remaining money in my bank account will cover these costs only when, and if, I can afford them. In all honesty, I don't like to spend money unless it's pre-planned and I know my budget can accommodate it. Shopping online is rarely conducive to that.

Why do you have multiple binders?

It's more for practicality than any other reason (although I like the colours!). I purchased one to begin with and it only had six envelopes that I concentrated on. Since my journey began, I have really noticed the advantage of saving over spending, which has meant more envelopes to fill. For example, instead of just one envelope that incorporates everyone's birthdays, I bought a second binder so there would be an envelope for every individual's birthday. When we decided to book our holiday, I wanted to be focused on those individual sinking funds attached to our trip so, *voilà*, binder three was introduced!

Do you take your binder out with you when you go shopping?

I have thought about it, but no, it stays at home in a safe place. I take the food shopping cash out of the binder and then put any unspent money back into the envelope. I find visiting it weekly really helps me remain focused and on track. If I carried it around, I might feel tempted to dip into additional envelopes and the spontaneous shopping habit might creep back in. I couldn't bear to lose the binder either!

Why don't you keep it in the bank to earn interest?

I would like to think I'm experiencing the best of both worlds right now, as I am saving in my binder and my bank account, something that wasn't happening before. When my card was in my hand, I would tap away without any care or thought, and with nothing left in the bank to make any interest on. Roll on to now and not only have I set aside savings for specific expenses, I can also see the money accruing in my bank.

What are you going to do when we go cashless?

At this moment, I have to admit I am dreading the possibility of ever becoming a cashless society. There are so many other factors to take into account before I worry about how I would save. I am more fearful over the homeless not getting a cup of coffee, those amazing Army veterans who stand proudly with poppies to sell each and every year, or the charity-donation pots on shop counters. What happens in those situations? I think it is a much bigger issue than the end of cash stuffing. I think it is the end of freedom, privacy and control.

Do you ever get tempted to dip into your binder for emergencies?

No, my individual envelopes are there for very important personal reasons, be it for Christmas gifts, my family's birthdays or to focus on next year's annual bills. Each one I've included ensures I'm not enduring one massive outgoing at any given time. By adding a socializing envelope, which I use for anything I wish to buy for myself, it's been great at preventing me from using other funds. I also have the just-in-case fund where I put a set amount in each month for anything else I may not have factored in or known about prior to that month. I once used the just-in-case money to purchase school shoes and it meant I remained focused whilst heading into town, knowing I only had £50 on me and no card. I didn't drift into any unplanned shops and start spending.

I really want to do this but I pay everything via direct debit. How can I make it work?

Do you have to pay everything by direct debit? I went through my bills and worked out what money would stay in the bank to pay the debits and how much I could take out for my cash savings and spends. I do have some annual bills that I have incorporated into my binder, such as car insurance, and water which is paid every six months. My savings goals are those things that aren't covered via direct debit, like our weekly food shop, birthdays, Christmas and any short-term savings, such as school uniform or holiday savings. Some people have incorporated hair, nails and even tattoos into their binders, all of which are not payable via direct debit.

What do you do with any money left over from your weekly food shop?

I save it! In the beginning, I wasn't comfortable committing to a certain amount for a savings challenge, but I felt something put aside was far better than nothing. So, once I had done my weekly food shop and top-up, I would be left with a small amount from my £90 budget. I decided to stick whatever was remaining into a separate envelope each week and open it up once I had been doing this for forty-five weeks. It wasn't a set amount so there was no pressure and whatever was left each week was a bonus. It quickly became an incentive to try and save £1100 with a plan to buy my husband a watch while we were away in the USA. After seven months, I had an incredible £940, which was more than enough for what I needed. The remaining food budget money was then added to a Christmas saving envelope.

What do I do with all the coins I have left?

When I first started this journey back in January 2022, I saved all my coins in a tub and used it towards holiday clothes for our youngest two. I now place it in a pot which we dip into as and when we need to. I don't get many coins remaining each week but 50p here and there soon adds up and it means I am not breaking into notes like I would have done in the past. Alternatively, take a look at some of the savings challenges I have included in the book as these are a great way to make your coins work for you.

You clearly have lots of money if you are able to go to America on holiday?

Holidays are a financial balancing act. Like so many others, we love going on holiday and, while it is a luxury, it is also a priority for us as a family. We make sacrifices in other areas to make sure we save enough money to go away every other year. We have family in Florida and we can combine this with one of our favourite destinations, a trip to Disneyworld, but this is not an annual event. There is no way we could afford to do it every year and we forgo other trips in the meantime. You can find some amazing deals on all sorts of holidays, so always give yourself enough time for thorough homework.

I've had to give up some luxuries such as hair and nails. How would you budget for these?

It's really important not to confuse budgeting with cutting back on little luxuries. In fact, I think when a budget is introduced it gives you the potential to free money up to spend on those things you enjoy, be that hair, makeup, clothes or holidays. Once you have control of your money and you understand exactly what you have, you can start prioritizing. You may not be able to get your hair and nails done as often as you would like, but life isn't perfect and neither are our bank balances.

How do you budget for clothes?

Thankfully, clothes shopping isn't something I do regularly, for me or the children. I buy them a good selection of clothes for birthdays and Christmas, and I don't really follow the latest fashion, LOL! If it is for an event or holiday, I take that into consideration beforehand and budget for it so this prevents me falling into a shopping frenzy. If this is a priority for you then factor this into your budget. I can also highly recommend eBay, charity shops and car boot sales to unearth some real gems.

Top five tips on starting budgeting?

1. Be honest with yourself about your spending habits.
2. Write down your income and any bills you have to pay each month.
3. Do not spread all the remaining income you have into saving pots.
4. Each month write a new budget to help you stay on track.
5. Check your calendar for any upcoming events to prevent any unplanned spends.

I want to start budgeting but should I wait until January?

No, don't wait until January. It isn't a New Year's resolution, which is often discarded before the month is out. Instead, start on your next pay day, be that weekly or monthly. You don't have to buy a binder or work out where every penny is going, you just need to set out a plan that's personal to your circumstances and get on with it. You have absolutely nothing to lose and possible savings to gain. We are brilliant at postponing things that could be seen as new or difficult, and they don't get any easier with delay. So, what are you waiting for?!

How do I get into this, I'm rubbish at saving?

There is only so much I can help you with. I wish I could be right by your side to cheer you on, but second best is this book and my musings on TikTok. What I will say, until I am purple in the face, is how simple this method of saving is. I found it hard sticking to a goal, be that weight loss, gym attendance or healthy eating, but it was fast results and seeing actual money sitting there in my binder at the end of each month that gave me all the motivation and confirmation I needed to continue. It sounds crazy when saying it out loud, but it's so much fun!

Resources

Citizens Advice

Previously known as the Citizens Advice Bureau back in my day, the information service began on 4th September 1939, the day after war was declared. Since then the independent national treasure has supported the population through war, recession, housing issues, unemployment, consumer affairs, Brexit and a pandemic. It is an invaluable resource for myriad queries, problems and concerns, including debt management, energy bills, family law and the cost-of-living crisis. From providing you with the latest on grants, benefits and compensation to helping you take your meter reading and giving legal advice, they have an open-door policy and are free to use. They also offer over-the-phone support if you do not have a branch local to you. Take a look at their website to see exactly what they do.

https://www.citizensadvice.org.uk/

MoneySavingExpert

All hail the amazing Mr Martin Lewis, a financial journalist and broadcaster, who founded his money-saving-advice website almost twenty years ago. Martin dedicates his time to sharing his considerable financial expertise in an accessible, informative and practical way. With his finger firmly on the government and money market pulses, he gives us real-time reports through social media, television and his website. Martin has a unique way of speaking to and for the people, which was evident when he tackled the energy crisis. It can be overwhelming when decisions are made around your money which are out of your control, so I would recommend this website. I find it hugely helpful because it is easy to navigate and is a great source of sensible tips and tools on anything from loans, consumer rights and insurance to mortgage rates and savings plans. As they state clearly, this is a journalistic website, so it is important to do your own research too, but this is a good place to start.

https://www.moneysavingexpert.com/

Money and Pensions Service

I found this by accident. I was on the hunt for information about what schools teach our children about money and budgeting, when I stumbled across this website and discovered they work alongside the Department of Work and Pensions. They offer five core functions: pension guidance, debt advice, money guidance, consumer protection and strategy. What jumped out at me was their Money Talk Week programme which offers an abundance of knowledge, including free information packs designed for families, schools and workplaces. If you struggle to have these sorts of conversations with family and friends, then the tools are there to help guide you in the right direction.

https://maps.org.uk/

Financial Professionals

A bit like the butcher, the baker and the candlestick maker, but in this instance the broker, the accountant and the bank manager. Let's start with the broker or adviser, a professional individual or company who liaises between 'buyer' and 'seller' to support a transaction and take a commission. They are a great way to find the best deal, whether it is for insurance, mortgages, pensions or stocks and shares. A word of caution: like any external person you share financial information with, you need to check their credentials. In the UK, financial advisers are regulated by the Financial Conduct Authority who set out rules for them to follow which will protect their clients.

It's the same with chartered accountants, who are either members of the ICAEW (Institute of Chartered Accountants in England and

Wales) or the ACCA (Association of Chartered Certified Accountants). If you have your own business or are self-employed, you may prefer to employ an accountant rather than tackle your own accounts and tax.

As for the bank manager, it feels like a character from the seventies rather than a position that is relevant today. Some may still have a direct relationship with their bank manager and can go to them for advice, but most likely your connection with your bank is online and through a vast call centre. You can be given an advisor when opening up an account in a local branch and their job is to guide and support you, so whilst the bank doors are still open their service is valuable. If you do not feel you are handling your bank account in the best way, then book yourself a meeting with your nearest branch and see what advice is available to you.

Friends and Family

Money is still a taboo subject amongst family and friends. We live in a culture where we often clam up about our financial woes and worry judgements will be thrust upon us. We need to be more relaxed about talking to those closest to us about money. I am not suggesting you tell people how much you earn, what you paid for your house or the size of your overdraft, but if you are finding the financial side of your life challenging, then it is good to share. Those who know you best may be able to help and advise in the most trustworthy, loving environment. I am well aware some will not have this support. I didn't for a long time, but now I am comfortable talking about money and, in turn, my family and friends are more open with me. Not one person has all the answers and we learn from each other. I hope there may be someone you can confide in and maybe you could help each other navigate through difficult times. Find a budget buddy to keep you on course.

Social Media

As you know, one post on TikTok changed my money mindset for ever. While it is called a social media platform, I prefer to call it a sharing platform. I am a big advocate for using it to find like-minded people, learn more about money matters, join support groups and discover real-life knowledge as people divulge their personal journeys and experiences. Would I have learned the method I use now if it hadn't been for social media? No. I am not saying this is the answer, but it is another resource that you can spend time investigating and you may just find the answer you are looking for. As for me, I strive to keep my content and social media page a safe place to ask questions and continue to build a community of people focused on being better with their money. If you don't have external support available or you are too nervous to reach out, then social media may be able to help. Your tribe is your vibe, after all.

Budget Buddies

I am not alone when it comes to finding a practical solution to money worries. I have been bowled over by the response to my cash stuffing journey on TikTok. I never imagined that so many people would have found me on the platform or taken control of their money using the method I share. It is brilliant to see how well others are doing and I love following their progress and celebrating their achievements. Here are just a few of the amazing comments I have received. If you still aren't sure this method is for you, have a read of the below. What better validation for the budgeting way of life?! (Names and locations have been changed.)

'This is the first month, probably ever, that I still had money remaining right before payday. I still can't believe it. We have managed to save nearly £500 last month. We've been making it a priority and it's so much fun.' (Sarah, Newcastle)

'It's amazing, I appreciate what I've saved so much more when I can physically see it.' (John, Cardiff)

'I'm a single mum and although money is a little tight at times, since seeing your videos I decided to give it a go. I'm definitely going to start saving and my plans are to take my little one to Disney.' (Anna, Essex)

'I can't thank you enough for your cash stuffing videos. I'm so excited to share with you that in one month alone I have saved £308. I'm truly amazed at myself. I'm planning a trip to New York next year and this is going to help me heaps.' (Michelle, Brighton)

'Just ordered my first binder. I can't wait to start getting organized with my spending. I'm due to go on maternity leave in a few months, so it's super important for us as a family to be prepared.' (Issy, Reading)

'I'm having a nightmare with food shopping. I overspend all the time. Using this binder is going to be so helpful to stop the urge to overspend and start saving.' (Clare, London)

'I'm totally amazed at what I've saved so far by doing my own money stashing.' (Roger, Birmingham)

'I've been doing this method for three months and I'm blown over by the amount I've saved. It's a no brainer.' (Tracy, Eastbourne)

'Your videos inspired me to get a binder and after my first month, despite my lowest pay in three years, I have quite a bit left over before my next payday.' (Nick, Sussex)

'Ahhh thank you! I was very inspired by your posts and I already feel more in control of Christmas.' (Alison, Dorset)

'Doing this and seeing actual money means it's real and not some invisible money tree that gets stripped each month.' (Lucy, Devon)

'Honestly, this is such a good idea. We used to do this at work and you see what you're spending and where. Using a card, you don't realize.' (Cath, Kent)

'I've been doing this for years. I used to be a waitress and it was the only way I could save all my cash. I recommend it to everyone I know.' (Nicki, Berkshire)

'Been doing this for three months now with my other half and we've literally saved so much between us. I just can't believe how much money was being wasted before.' (John, Manchester)

'After finding your page, I also started saving and in a few months I had the children's uniform cost all set aside with time and money to spare. Normally I'd be panicking throughout the holidays wondering how I was going to afford it all.' (Miranda, Suffolk)

'Before cash stuffing, I couldn't even get through the month on my earnings. I've now booked a holiday and purchased a second-hand car all because I've used this method.' (Elaine, Surrey)

'I never used to plan for anything. I had the 'you only live once' attitude. Feel so much more in control and my money spreads further. I started in July and I budget every month now. I haven't touched the remaining money in my bank account to use for Christmas presents.' (Belinda, Dublin)

'I've been inspired by you and your journey and I've seen my own finances improve.' (Craig, Northampton)

'I started using the same method as you and I've just cleared my credit card debt. In eight months I will be clear of all debts and £700 a month better off.' (Susie, Peterborough)

'It's funny but I can't believe how much stress has been removed from our life as a family since doing this. I no longer worry about birthdays and Christmas. The best part is, we are now in a position to book a family holiday abroad.' (Susannah, London)

Acknowledgements

The notion that my budget journey has been turned into a book remains a 'pinch me' moment. I wouldn't be in this position if it wasn't for so many amazing people who have guided me along the way. It's hard to sum up my gratitude in words, but I am going to try, so apologies if this sounds like an Oscar acceptance speech! Imagine me saying this while wearing a fabulous gown . . .

To my brilliant agent, Emily Sweet, who saw something in me I didn't know was possible, your expertise and handholding have kept me safe and grounded throughout this unfamiliar process. Thank you times a million. To the Quercus publishing family, you made me feel welcome from our very first meeting and especially to Katy Follain, my editor with the beautiful soul. Thank you for supporting me throughout and putting together the best, most hard-working team a girl could wish for, including Nina Sandelson, Lipfon Tang, Lizzie Dorney-Kingdom and Chloë Johnson-Hill. You took my vision and ran with it. Huge thanks also to Amber Anderson for bringing the book to life with the most fantastic illustrations. And to Lucy Brazier, my guardian angel, you now have a special place in my heart. You worked on this with me throughout and gave me the courage to use my voice and tell my story. Thank you for being my sidekick and inspiration.

To my hero, my husband and best friend, Nick. Thank you for absolutely everything. You may have questioned your choice of life partner at times – especially when it comes to my cooking – but what a life we've created together. You see something in me I am yet to see in myself and your belief in me is what has kept me going. We are, and always will be, each other's biggest cheerleaders. I value everything about you and more. You really are the most amazing man in the entire world.

To my darling eldest daughter Lacey, thank you for showing me a different kind of love, as a Mum and now a Nanna to Luna and Alfie. If I can inspire you to be and do anything, it is to believe in yourself and know that your beautiful heart and caring nature will serve you well in life. I'm so unbelievably proud of you, my firstborn love. So, to my gorgeous second daughter, Ava, who brightens up the room with her humour and intelligence. You have such amazing morals and are destined for great things. You are golden to me. And to my youngest daughter, my precious Poppy, you amaze everyone with your courage and fearlessness, and you put 100% into everything regardless of the outcome. Don't be scared to be different, you deserve to shine bright like the diamond you are. I love the three of you beyond measure.

To my Mum and G-pa, I love you guys so much. Thank you for accepting me for who I am, supporting my decisions and celebrating my achievements. Who would have thought I would write a book,

Mum?! Thank you for your generosity and bravery in allowing me to share our story.

To my mother and father-in-law, Belinda and Steve, you are amazing, selfless and caring. Steve, your words of wisdom are greatly appreciated and I take on board every piece of knowledge you share. Belinda, you are our very own Mary Poppins with your many talents and unconditional love for us all. The best couple I know!

To my siblings, I'm so glad and lucky to have you in my life. Thank you for never giving up on me. I know my strong opinions may have tested your patience over the years, but they are always spoken with love and passion. We've all taken different paths, but I will never forget the early journey we shared together.

And finally, to my wonderful TikTok followers and budgeting buddies. It's because of you this opportunity has become a reality, so I want to thank you all for your support and allowing me the safe place to be my authentic self. You have helped make finances fun. I am overwhelmed and humbled by it all. Thank you for being there and here's to what lies ahead.

BUDGET TRACKER	MONTH:	

INCOME	OUTGOING	TOTAL £
	(DIRECT DEBITS)	£
	(TRANSPORT/FUEL)	£
	(FOOD)	£
TOTAL INCOME: £	TOTAL OUTGOINGS: £	REMAINING BALANCE: £

BUDGET BINDER

SINKING FUND (BIRTHDAY, CLOTHING, HOLIDAY)	GOAL/TARGET AMOUNT	EACH WEEK/MONTH CONTRIBUTION

TOTAL £